Dreaming in Indian

Dreaming in Indian
Contemporary Native American Voices

Edited by
Lisa Charleyboy and Mary Beth Leatherdale

annick press
toronto • new york • vancouver

LET'S JOIN HANDS

Cover collage by Inti Amaterasu with images from Ishmil Waterman, Denise Payette, Kit Thomas and Chamisa Edd

Interior Design by Inti Amaterasu

Annick Press Ltd.

We acknowledge the support of the Canada Council for the Arts, the Ontario Arts Council, and the Government of Canada through the Canada Book Fund (CBF) for our publishing activities.

ONTARIO ARTS COUNCIL
CONSEIL DES ARTS DE L'ONTARIO
50 YEARS OF ONTARIO GOVERNMENT SUPPORT OF THE ARTS
50 ANS DE SOUTIEN DU GOUVERNEMENT DE L'ONTARIO AUX ARTS

Cataloging in Publication
  Dreaming in Indian : Contemporary Native American voices / edited by Lisa Charleyboy and Mary Beth Leatherdale.

Includes bibliographical references and index.
Issued in print and electronic formats.
ISBN 978-1-55451-687-2 (bound).--
ISBN 978-1-55451-689-6 (pdf).--ISBN 978-1-55451-688-9 (epub)

     1. Native artists--Canada--Biography--Juvenile literature.
2. Indian artists--United States--Biography--Juvenile literature.
I. Leatherdale, Mary Beth, editor of compilation II. Charleyboy, Lisa, editor of compilation

N6549.5.A54D74 2014   j704.03'97   C2014-900856-2
                                                 C2014-900857-0

Distributed in Canada by:
Firefly Books Ltd.
50 Staples Avenue, Unit 1
Richmond Hill, ON L4B 0A7

Published in the U.S.A. by Annick Press (U.S.) Ltd.
Distributed in the U.S.A. by:
Firefly Books (U.S.) Inc.
P.O. Box 1338
Ellicott Station
Buffalo, NY 14205

Printed in China

Visit us at: **www.annickpress.com**

Visit Lisa Charleyboy at: **www.lisacharleyboy.com**

Also available in e-book format. Please visit www.annickpress.com/ebooks.html for more details. Or scan

For all the Indigenous youth in NDN country
— strive and thrive! — L.C.

For Ben and Sarah, who always want to
know more — M.B.L.

CONTENTS

FOREWORD

"If your imagination isn't working—and, of course, in oppressed people that's the first thing that goes—you can't imagine anything better. Once you can imagine something different, something better, then you're on your way."

I said this about Indigenous youth many years ago. At that time, I and many others were struggling writers looking for "a good book to fall into." Sadly, some of those women are gone now, before they had a chance to create their own good stories. Some of us hung in there, becoming teachers, healers, lawyers, and, myself, a writer.

The writers and artists in *Dreaming in Indian* made it home, to ourselves, to our medicines, to our beliefs, to our stories, to our art, and to our music, and we did so with extraordinary alacrity, strength, resilience, and awesome talent. We braided the art of the external to our own. We dug inside the depths of our rage until peace, love, and struggle were born. We scraped together our music, scrabbled for language that would express our deepest sentiments, our strongest desires, and we expressed them.

All the works in the following pages are part of that amazing struggle to go forward, into modernity, onto the global stage, without leaving our ancient selves behind.

The pages of this book carry their ancestors with them. They carry the incredible heroism of the silent years, those years when resistance and our beliefs, our stories, were whispered in hushed tones, in curtained humble homes, in gasps, between the punitive and prohibitive power of colonialism. They carry extraordinary visuals in colors as bright as Norval Morrisseau could invent, to illuminate our very souls.

They sing out loud in verses, plain and compelling. They cry freedom in words commanding and unapologetic. They do so with tender insistence, bravery, and beauty.

Led by the great wave of writers of the new millennium, with art and music as their devoted companions, the contibutors in *Dreaming in Indian* call youth to rise, to return to our fold, and to fall into this "good book." Imagine a better world. Imagine yourself on the center stage of this continent. Let us all go forward into the future, bound to our ancient selves and as modern as any other.

Lee Maracle (Salish and Cree Stó:lō Nation)
Poet, Author, Instructor in the Aboriginal Studies Department at the University of Toronto

WELCOME

This book stemmed from a desire to showcase the real life of Indigenous people. Not the life portrayed in mainstream media and certainly not the life of Native people as it is seen through the lens of Hollywood. We wanted to give people a fresh perspective on what it means to be Native in North America. Both of us personally know how many amazingly talented Native American youth are out there doing great work and the ways in which they are often overlooked and their voices aren't heard. We wanted to give them a chance to tell their stories, their way.

But even we were blown away by the submissions of tremendous writing, artwork, and photographs, and by the generosity with which people shared their talents. You're in for an incredible treat and we're extremely grateful for each and every act of participation to make this project happen.

As you read through the book you'll notice that along with contributors' names, we've asked them to share their nations and home reserves. Contributors decided for themselves how to define their heritage. That choice to define who you are and what the future holds for you is what this book is all about.

Lisa and Mary Beth
Editors

"There is no one Indigenous perspective ...
no one Indigenous story. We are tremendously diverse peoples with
tremendously diverse life experiences. We are not frozen in the past,
nor are we automatically just like everybody else. That is why it is
so important for everyone to share their own story. In revealing their
personal truths, they help us all gain a better appreciation for the
messy, awesome, fun reality of the world we live in."

Wab Kinew (Anishinaabe)
Journalist, Hip hop artist, Director of Indigenous
Inclusion at the University of Winnipeg

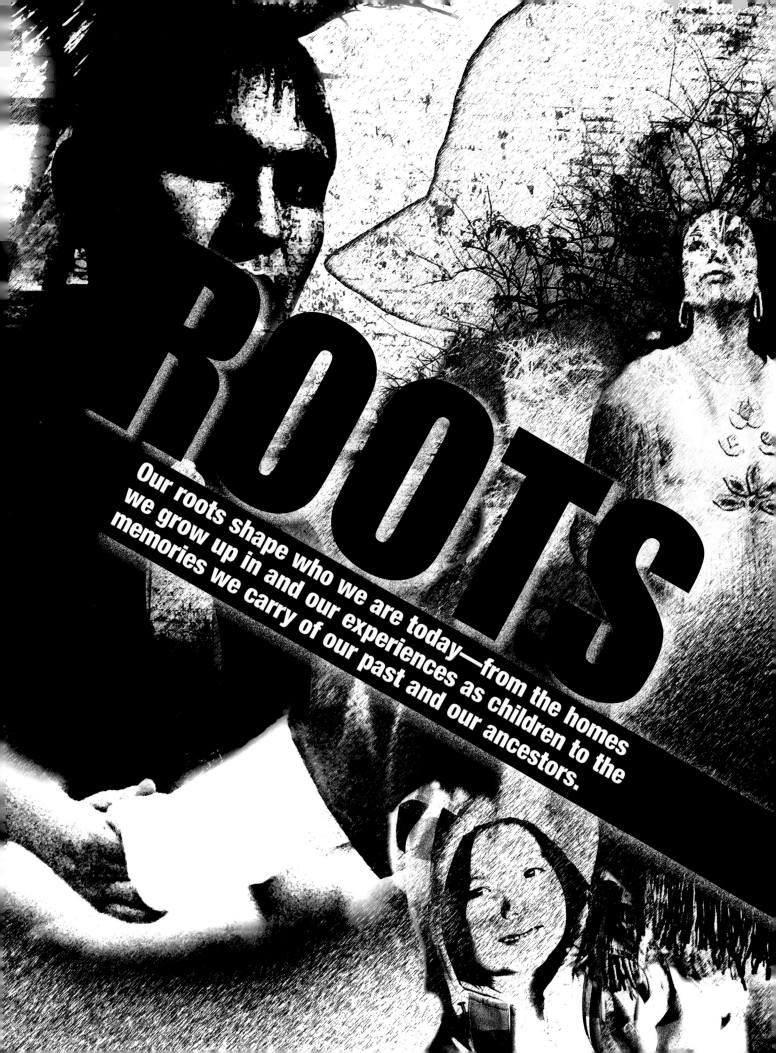

ROOTS

Our roots shape who we are today—from the homes we grow up in and our experiences as children to the memories we carry of our past and our ancestors.

I REMEMBER

Lullabies

So many nights I sat awake
and listened.

Old Mom, you were speaking
Nle7kepmxcin, Nsilxcin
with the many old ones
who came through our door.

I sat quietly, sometimes.
Sometimes, I pestered you
with questions.

Belly warm with toast,
Red Rose tea,
Pacific cream
and sugar.

I sat tracing designs
with my fingers on the
red and white tablecloth,
black and white benches.

Listening carefully to grandmother
voices, stories only heard in the quiet hours
between Elders.

"My girl, go to bed!"
"Baby, you're asking too many questions!"

Nle7kepmxcin,
Nsilxcin,
English.

I could never decide when one ended
and the next began,
lulled to sleep by an Indian lullaby.

Your voice soothing,
singing, praying,
and gently explaining.

"When it is your time, baby girl . . .
you will understand."

NICOLA CAMPBELL
(Nle7kepmx [Thompson], Nsilx [Okanagan], and Métis)
Artwork by Jessica Harjo (Otoe-Missouria Tribe and Osage/Pawnee/Sac & Fox)

Fried Bologna and Rice

At Auntie's house
we soak hides in the river,
soften them
in brains until they stink.

Peee-yew!

Then string them up,
stretched and tanned
in smoke.

And fried bologna and rice
is a feast
at Auntie's house.
We three *snunkwe schememeyt*,
we three childhood friends
drink Freshie.

Freshie, fried bologna,
and rice and Auntie's fry bread
has two holes in it,

one for me,
one for you.

Auntie always wears her hat
covered with buttons and pins,
angels, turtles, and

Bingo!

She sits in the corner by her lamp,
with scissors she cuts her hide,

snip, snip, snnnip!

We three *snunkwe schememeyt*,
we work hard at Auntie's house,
making bread,
making pies,
and beading flower necklaces.

" Our community was poor at that time; there was no venison and there was no fish to supplement it so we had to eat this canned meat over and over again. But I can remember being small, being around eight or nine years of age, stamping my feet and raising my hands up in the air and making a proclamation that if I ever have it within my way I'll never have anything to do with this meat ever, ever again. "

4
RESERVATION FOOD GROUPS

KEESIC DOUGLAS

**(OJIBWAY, MNJIKANING FIRST NATION)
MEMORY FROM HIS FATHER, MARK DOUGLAS,
WHOSE TRADITIONAL NAME IS BIIDAANKWAD
(CLOUD APPROACHING)**

THE PLACE I CALL
HOME

Welcome to the Arctic and the Inuit community of Pangnirtung, Nunavut, population 1,300.

Photos by **David Kilabuk** (Inuk)

H♡ME

Youth from across North America share their thoughts on home.

Nowhere, U.S.A.

It's the last place I fell asleep. By the shore of a dirty lake, I spent the night on the concrete steps wrapped tight in a sweater with a broken zipper. The place where I fell asleep after a lifetime awake in the essence of insanity, where I relaxed after I accepted your insanity, where I refused to fight it anymore. This is not a place. This is not a residence. It's an idea or it's a time. I fell headfirst into this stream of thought that many others had discovered while fishing for concepts, so it hits me like an arrow to the knee. Everything I ever thought before was a preconceived notion. The things they said were important have never made sense because they weren't important to me.

Some call it growing up. Some call it maturity. Some call it, and some call it, and some call it—
I cannot be the only one who thinks that this is home. That is where my heart is, after all.

Zach Medicine-Shield
(Blackfoot, Siksika Nation)

Monsoon Grass, Darrell Yazzie Jr. (Dine), Klagetoh, Arizona, U.S.A.

Flat Bay Tipi, Newfoundland, Canada, Shannon Webb-Campbell (Qualipu Mi'kmaq Federation of Newfoundland Indians)

Sunrise Awakening, Darrell Yazzie Jr. (Dine), Klagetoh, Arizona, U.S.A.

Home is where I was shaped by singers and weavers. Shaped by words and comments. Shaped by care and companionship. Home is a place I will never let go.

Lia Hart

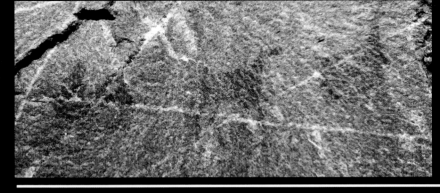

Agawa Pictographs, Sault Ste. Marie, Ontario, Canada, Denise Payette (Mississaugi First Nation)]

I run through you,
And I can feel your stories in me,
As if I've been here for thousands of years.
Iniskim calls me home—
Home, where I roam.
There's no buffalo to rub that stone,
The waters clean the blood up off this land.
I run through you,
And feel the spirits that once lived here,
Because this is home
Where we roam.

Julia Shaw
(Cree, Peepeekisis Nation)

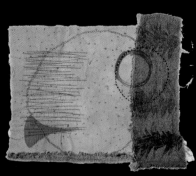

**Home, Alana McLeod
(Cree and Scottish)**

**Family Is Home, Browning, Montana, U.S.A., Adrienne Tailfeathers
(Blackfeet Nation, Aamsskaapipikani)**

To those who bullied me

oday is Pink Shirt day at my daughter Naia's school. All the kids wore pink to send the message that bullying won't be tolerated. I'm happy that bullying has a negative social stigma these days. It wasn't like that when I was a kid growing up in Cambridge Bay, Nunavut.

But today, I would personally like to thank everyone who bullied me as a child. I used to come home

Internationally renowned Inuk throat singer **Tanya Tagaq Gillis**

with frozen phlegm in my hair from being spit on. I was scared every day at recess and after school. I would get kicked, slapped, shoved, punched, berated, and put down.

I thank all of you who tormented me for teaching me resilience and that the world is not an easy place. Later in life, I came to understand more and feel compassion for those who have a hard life and think the only solution is to take it out on others.

You also taught me to not care what everyone thought of me. Without you, my childhood bullies, I would have been bullied into stopping singing by haters. Many tried to make me feel shame for what comes from my heart.

Again, thank you, bullies, because of you I am STRONG!

Lakota Thunder

Dana Hillestad
(Lakota)

Thunder is sounding behind the fields and lightning

Is making a path to the corn rows

The atmosphere is charged,

The coffee cold; I remember

They told me Great-Grandmother's name was Thunder

A clap makes the hair on my arms raise and quiver

The screen slams;

She is always here, making herself known

More coffee and a quick look out

On the porch

I shut my eyes tight, the dirt is stinging

I remember them saying,

Big Thunder could pray a storm up,

Make an evil man

Fall in love, and twist the sheets dry on the line

All from another county

Even one hundred years later,

Thunder can rock this house and

Get me on the hooked-rug praying

She plays rough

The women in this family

Have always been strong

Like Sioux women warriors

I wonder

Can she see the jagged lines of black streak down

While I wipe my cheek with your old shirt,

Rub my belly, peel another peach.

Artwork "From Me to You" detail by LauraLee K. Harris (First Nations mixed ancestry)

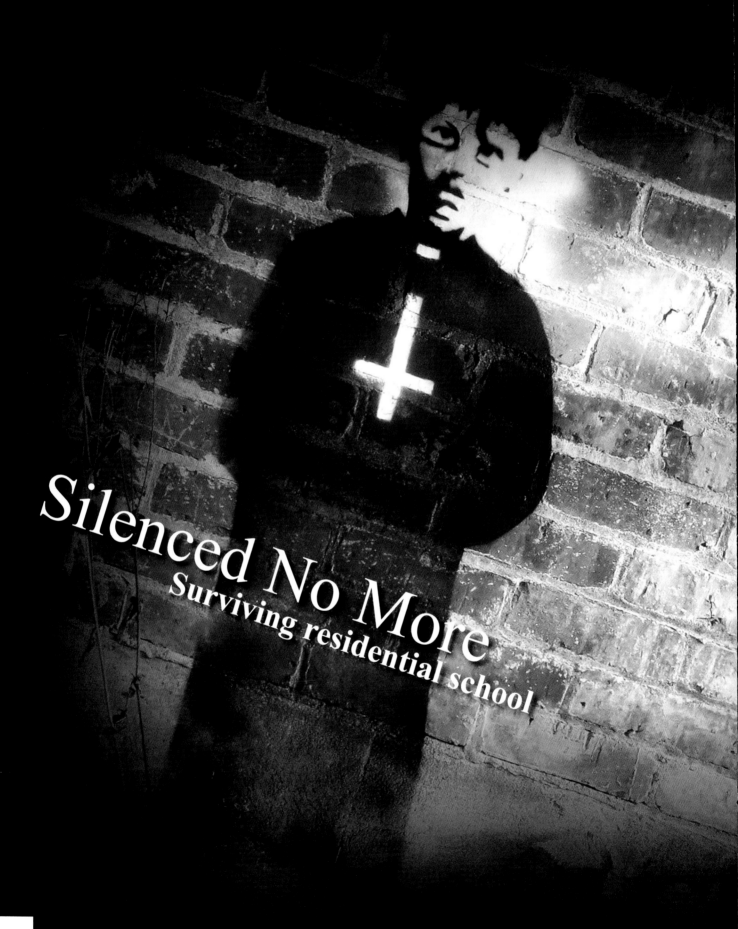

Silenced No More
Surviving residential school

Graffiti on the St. Michael's Residential School in
Alert Bay, British Columbia
Photographs by Kim Peterson
(Kwakwaka'wakw,
Namgis First Nation)

My Mother's Teachings

Isabelle Knockwood (Mi'kmaq)

Dear Children, Grandchildren, and Great-Grandchildren,

My mother was my first teacher. Her teachings are as relevant to me today as a great-grandmother as they were to me decades ago when I was a toddler. No matter what happened throughout my lifetime, whether good or not, her stories have sustained me. Twelve years of residential indoctrination could not even erase or replace my mother's early influence.

I am Mi'kmaq. I attended the Indian Residential School in Shubenacadie, Nova Scotia, for twelve years. Approximately two thousand Mi'kmaw and Maliseet children attended the school from 1929 to 1967. During those thirty-eight years, over three generations of Aboriginal people were denied the basic human rights of freedom of speech and religion.

In 1867, the British North America Act stated Canada's goal, "Our country's goal is to destroy the tribal society and assimilate Indians into the white dominant society as quickly as it is convenient." Why was it so important to destroy tribal society? Tribal society consists of people who have common ancestors, speak a common language, and live in a common region. The Mi'kmaq and Maliseet belong to the Wabanaki Confederacy. The other three members of the Wabanaki Confederacy are the Abenaki, Passamaquoddy, and Penobscot. We are known as the Wabanaki people by other First Nations because we are the first people on Turtle Island to see the white light known as the dawn.

The Wabanaki First Nations have common Aboriginal ancestors and speak different dialects of the same language, whose sounds are rooted in the Mother tongue called Algonquin. Our Aboriginal ancestors occupied the northeast forest region of Turtle Island. We call our ancestral land Turtle Island, but the Europeans renamed it North America.

True to its objective to assimilate Indians, residential schooling removed everything familiar to us in an effort to make us like White people. Residential schooling took everything, including my family and community, my culture and traditional teachings, as well as my heritage. In doing so, it destroyed my Aboriginal identity and left me alone to face the threat of annihilation unarmed and unprotected. I stood naked, isolated, and silenced in a world not of my making, and my parents were made powerless to protect me. They were placed on lands put in trust of the federal government with no human rights and no freedoms. By definition, Indigenous First Nations were prisoners of war, and, by extension, their children attending residential schools became child warriors struggling to stay alive by

whatever means they were able to muster. As a child warrior, I had to fight to keep alive. I was taught every day that I was not a person, that I had no right to speak Mi'kmaq, and that my ancestors were savages and heathens who had no god, no religion, no political structure, and no laws.

When I was six or seven or eight years old, I went home for summer vacation and I asked my mother, "Mom, do Indians have a god?"

She replied, "What makes the grasses grow and what makes the trees grow makes you grow." I looked at the green grasses and the tall trees and I noticed my own growth and I understood Creation.

My second question was, "Mom, what does living in harmony with nature mean?"

She said, "When the seasons change, we change." And when I observed the seasons, and heard the winds, and noticed myself growing, I began to understand growth and evolution.

And finally, I had one more question: "Mom, why do we greet the dawn?"

She said, "We greet the dawn because we are the People of the Dawn. We are the first ones to see the white light coming to announce the sunrise, and when the sun comes up, it gives us light and we are able to see where we are going and we are able to work,

and the sun gives us warmth and the Elders feel better and are able to move around. There is magic everywhere," she added, "like when the sun and moon are in the sky at the same time on the full moon, it's magic."

My mother's teachings made me the person I am today—creative, productive, and responsible. I hope that the teachings I pass on to you today will also sustain you in your future and make you creative and productive as well as responsible for your actions.

Residential Schools in North America

From the late 1800s to as recently as the 1970s in Canada, the Canadian and American governments forced First Nations and Native American children to attend Christian boarding or residential schools. About 150,000 Aboriginal, Inuit, and Métis children living in Canada and 100,000 Native Americans living in the United States were taken from their families and communities and forced to abandon their Native language and culture. The physical, emotional, and sexual abuse that children endured at the schools caused trauma that for many survivors led to violence, addiction, or suicide and continues to haunt the generations that follow.

My brother Xavier and I took my niece Tessa on a boat ride on the Attawapiskat River. Xavier was leaving the next day for school, and Tessa was staying in Attawapiskat with her mother. ■

This photo of kids doing the round dance at the powwow reminds me of my sisters. My sisters used to hold hands when they were younger and sang this song all the time, but now I don't see kids doing that as much these days. ■

This is my friend's dog, Shogun. We took him for a ride out to the bay. He wouldn't stop jumping all over me. ■

The Virgin Mary stands at the church that I went to with my grandparents. I'd see the Virgin Mary on my way to work at the hospital, on my breaks, and when I'd leave. My grandmother used to tell me when I was younger that Virgin Mary was also my mother and that I should always look up to her when I am lost. ■

Leaving Home
Saying good-bye to Attawapiskat

My niece visits every day at my parents' place. I always enjoy her company. This is the last time I saw her before I left. ▪

I was out hiking with my dog (half wolf, half German shepherd) and we met this bear. The bear didn't attack or anything. We just minded our own business and continued to walk home. ▪

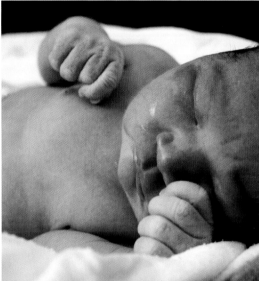

My brother Xavier and some friends and I were on a three-hour hike and we took a break to have a cigarette. We came back with a lot of mosquito bites. ▪

This is the church I used to attend with my grandparents. I took the shot while my mother and I were waiting for my father and siblings to come home from his camp. I lost count of how many hours I was there with her. That was a good day with my mother. We just talked about things, how I would spend my life out of Attawapiskat, and had a few laughs here and there.

Priscella Rose (Attawapiskat First Nation)

I left my home in Attawapiskat to go to school in Moosonee. My favorite thing about Attawapiskat is that my family lives there. All my friends live there. I also love the nature. And I love the winter season. There are a lot of activities, such as sledding, broomball, and hockey.

Indians in the City

Henry Heavy Shield
(Kainai [Blood] First Nation)

This is about an Indian boy who moved to the city. Well, he wasn't really a boy anymore. More like a young man. So this young man moved from his Reserve to a big city to go to school. He lived there for an entire year and yet he still couldn't understand why he felt so empty inside. "This city is beautiful. How can you not like it here?" people often asked him. They pointed out the mountains and the ocean and the fresh air that danced and rolled in between.

"I like it," the young man would say. "It's just that I can't help but miss my home." He saw Indians every now and again, at school, on the bus, at the grocery store, and sometimes he would nod at them. Or sometimes they would pass each other on the street, not saying a word, but always looking each other in the eye, acknowledging something they each knew but couldn't explain.

But people soon took the young man's longing for home as a weakness. "He's just not cut out for this place," they'd say. And it wasn't long before their "hellos" and "how-are-you-doings" became less and less frequent, until they eventually stopped altogether. The young man didn't let any of this discourage him, of course. He kept himself busy as best he could and he worked hard on his studies. What surprised the young man, however, was that he found a way to turn this longing into a strength. All he had to do was close his eyes and think about the Reserve. He felt like a giant tree whenever he imagined that he was home. It was during these moments that he felt his roots search deep into the land, sucking up water and nutrients and love, everything that he needed to survive.

However, the city took its toll on his imagination, and his memory began to fray. He still felt like a tree most of the time, but more like a tree growing on the face of a cliff, one whose roots must burrow deep into the cracks in the rocks. This type of tree grows flat and spindly, but, still, it manages to survive. This is exactly how the young man felt as he walked at the feet of the tall, concrete buildings, searching for a place that felt even just a little bit like home.

CONCRETE INDIANS

Capturing the Indian Urban Experience **Nadya Kwandibens**

(Anishinaabe, French, Northwest Angle #37 First Nation)

STARBUCKS COFFEE

STARBUCKS COFFEE

PRIVATE PROPERTY
**NO PARKING
IN DRIVEWAY**

Jennifer Podemski | Toronto, ON | May 2008

Lisa Charleyboy | Toronto, ON | November 2008

Dundas

37

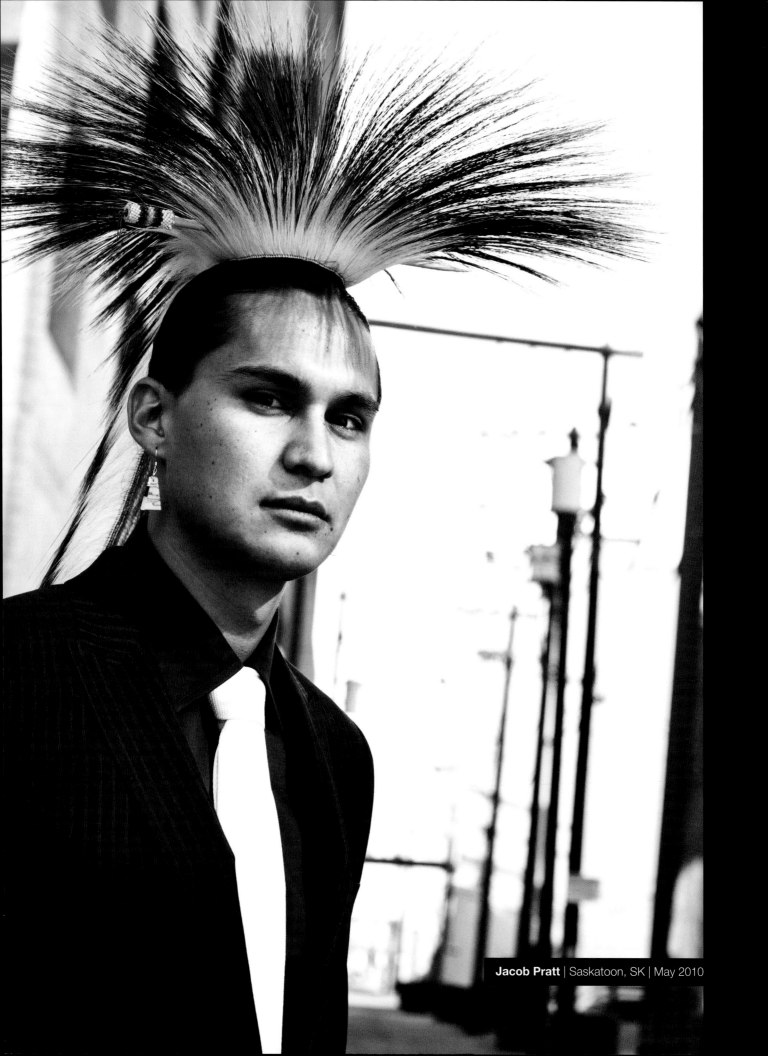

Jacob Pratt | Saskatoon, SK | May 2010

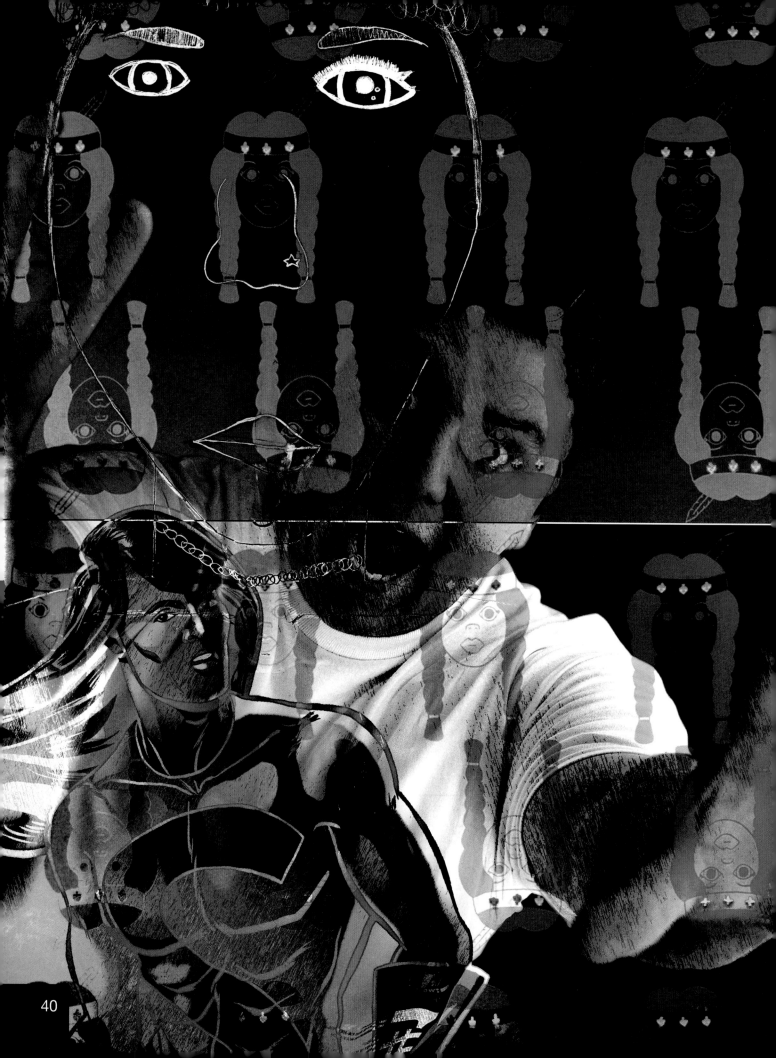

BATTLES

Encounters with racism and stereotyping, issues of gender identity and equality, abuse, addiction, and poverty are just some of the battles that Native American youth face.

GROWING UP WITH POCAHONTAS

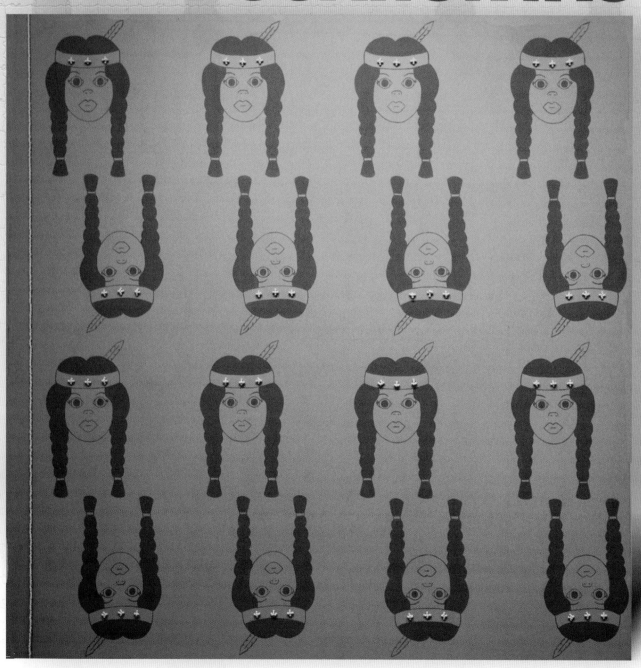

Indian Doll painting by **Kelli Clifton**

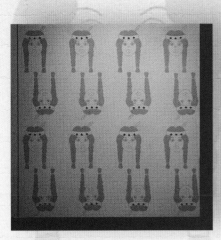

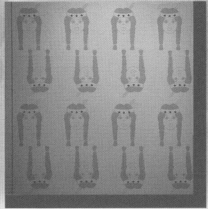

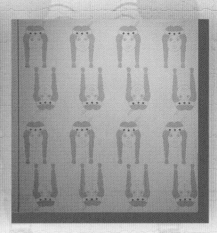

Charlotte Logan
(Akwesasne Mohawk)

The Disney Pocahontas was really popular when I was in high school. That's when that movie came out. The character was made in the image of the beautiful Native actress Irene Bedard. So when someone says you look just like Pocahontas, it's not meant as an insult. But because our history is left out of any teaching of history in the U.S., it's all they know of me. When I match that image it's super exciting for them. I know they mean well, but they're pigeonholing me as a person. It's complicated. So I don't think it's an insult when people tell me I look like Pocahontas. Even Natives say it to me. Sometimes I get annoyed. But I try to take it as a compliment and understand it's coming from a place of ignorance. Any negativity associated with it is because people don't know our history.

Alida Kinnie Starr
(Mixed Blood Mohawk)

Pocahontas doesn't mean much to me, aside from when I learned that because she was fair-skinned and young she was chosen as an example of our women as a method of swaying upper-class Europeans who were afraid to make their way to America because of the so-called heathens here. Then I found her story more interesting. But when I was a little kid, I thought she was just a Disney character and not a real person.

But the stereotyping of Native women used to affect me a lot. I sometimes felt like if I didn't wear cultural signifiers like beaded earrings and bone chokers that Natives would judge me for not being "a real Indian." Often at Native events, if I am going onstage, the producers have requested that I wear "Native jewelry" and have my hair straightened to look more typically Indian. I have also seen many artists being "bronzed" before we get on camera.

I was more insecure about being mixed blood when I was in my twenties. These days, I care less about markers like that. What people think about me doesn't change who I am.

Kelli Clifton
(Tsimshian)

The first time I watched *Pocahontas*, I was in my mid-teens. Although the movie had been out for years, my parents didn't allow me to watch it as a child. Even as a teenager aware of the horrific racism in both real life and fairy tales, I couldn't help but become mesmerized with this cartoon depiction of a Native woman. She was everything that the Aboriginal woman seen on the nightly news wasn't. She could sing, she could swim, she gathered food, she was confident, the boys loved her—but most important, she had dark skin and dark hair, just like me.

Ever since I was a child, I've had a fascination with the Indian dolls you find in tourist shops. Even though these objects do not accurately represent the majority of today's First Nations peoples, both tourists and people of First Nations ancestry value them. They often appeared in my relatives' homes. My painting *Indian Doll* is a comment on the allure of these stereotypical yet charming dolls.

What IS Gender?

Aja Sy
(Ojibway Anishinaabe,
Lac Seul First Nation)

Gender is a ridicule.
A personal tag.
A word to describe you.
How you are supposed to be.
Almost a stereotype.

When someone defines it,
When they disrupt it,
Drown it,
Sink the ship,
They're a disgrace.

Why is our society
So programmed this way?
What if this is who you really are?
Not the programmed but the
programmer.
Programmer of gender.
Of who we really are.

We all need some programming.
All.

What if the world didn't have gender?
What would people be like?
What would they do, say, or like?
How would they act?
Who would they be?
What if our lives were turned upside
down?
For just a day or two.
What would we be?

Not Girl, Boy, Man, Woman,
Transgendered.

What are we really?
We are Human.

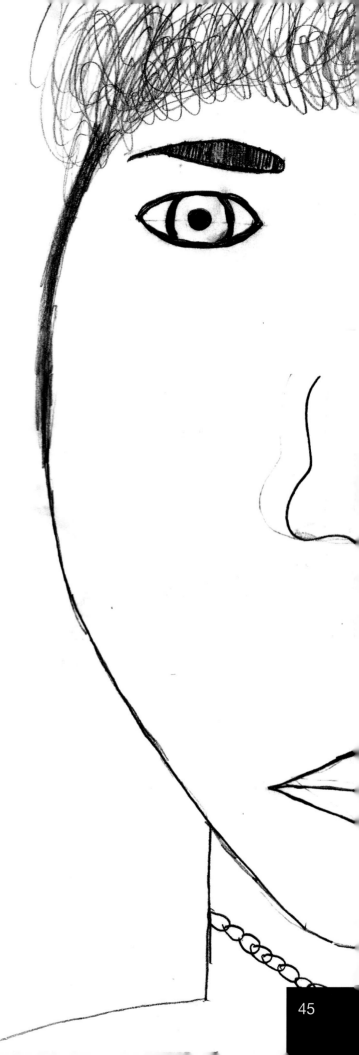

My Reality

Karina Rain Dominguez
(Hopi, Navajo, Mayan)

Developing into a woman by age nine

Men loved to commit the worst crime

Wandering hands knew how to open
the door

And make my body feel like the
earthquake of '94

Good thing a knife through flesh

Was able to hold back one creep's
underage caress

Funny, I wondered why numerous
narcotics

Wouldn't blur memories caused by a
handful of psychotics

Wanting to "check out," there were tries
after tries

But death never won the prize

Time turned me into one of the "lost"
kids on Skid Row

If an undercover was around, learned
which route to go

So, don't be deceived by these glasses,
my dear

My smiling self may be aiming for a
legitimate career

Just trust I've already experienced
some of the rawest realities

Since the Department of Child and
Family Services took me from my family

ARTIST

TOM GREYEYES

(NAVAJO NATION) CREATES
SITE-SPECIFIC GRAFFITI
INSTALLATIONS, VIDEO ART,
AND PRINTS THAT CHALLENGE
THE STEREOTYPICAL IDEAS OF
NATIVE PEOPLES IN AMERICA.

CULTURE CLASHES

RUN WITH THE HERD

BLUE BUFFALO

PROTECT THE SACRED
DON'T LOOK BACK

YOUTH ELDER
WAH WHEAT PASTE

PROPS H2O is LIFE

The Only Place She Knows

Tonya-Leah Watts
(Wikwemikong Unceded Indian Reserve)

I trace the lines of his body and he leans over and kisses my cheek. I have once again achieved that look in his eye, like a craving that has finally been fulfilled. Then, leaving the bills rolled up and bound with elastic, he puts on his suit and tie and leaves.

My name is Evangeline and I'm twenty-four years old. I haven't been blessed with the wits to go to college, get a job, and "assimilate" into the white world as they planned for me to do. No. I've been blessed with a beautiful body though . . . the only thing I've learned to use in order to get my next meal. Maybe, I did have a good working brain once. I mean, I'll never know. I haven't seen my real friends and family since I was being driven away in the back of an old truck, bumping and rolling its way to my hell. Confined in a white building with dull walls, dull tasteless food, and dull classrooms with the bold letters "LOOKING UNTO JESUS" across the top of every blackboard, I realized that I had lost everything I had once known. I think that I could've managed if I wasn't scrutinized for speaking the only words I knew. If I didn't have to sleep with one eye open, hoping that the man in the white robe didn't pick me at nighttime. If I didn't have to walk with my head down, shamed for being the color I am.

When I finally got out, it was no better. My life dragged on. I was a bottom-feeder of society. I still had to walk with my head down in daylight because if I did happen to look up, there was always that one person that gave me that look to put me back in my place. That's when I learned that as the night wore on, and the beer rounds got higher and higher, the color of my skin didn't matter anymore. And so I would pick one, give them what they wanted, and in return they gave me what I needed. And so here I am now, catching a bite to eat and keeping to the shadows in the daytime. When night comes, I pick my next prey.

Tonight, it's a Friday. They'll be generous with the cash. First things first. I need a new outfit. I see a woman about my size walk out of a high-end fashion store, a large box containing what must be some kind of boots in her right hand and a bag of clothes in her left. I walk right behind her on the busy sidewalk and wait for her to look to her right. Then I snatch the first thing I can out of the bag before blending back into the crowd. I get to the public bathroom in the subway and I realize I've struck gold. I slip on the dress, a tight bold purple material covered with sequins, stopping about five inches above the knee. It accents all the right parts and complements my copper skin. I open my purse, which carries everything I own, and pull out the usual: lipstick, mascara, eyeliner, blush, shadow, and some stolen perfume. My hand brushes something at the bottom of my purse, and I take it out—a necklace

The neon signs color the city, and my hunt begins.

with a small wooden bear that my father carved for me. Mkoons, meaning "little bear"; it was my name before I was taken to the residential school where they changed it to "Evangeline." The necklace was the only thing from my past that I managed to keep hidden, the only thing that reminds me of my home, of who I am, or who I was.

The moon takes its place, the neon signs color the city, and my hunt begins. I choose a bar and immediately find him. Hair ruffled from him constantly running his hands through it in frustration, tie loosened, slouched, and a disappointed scowl on his face. I watch as he orders a few strong shots. The first couple he takes stiffly, grimacing at its fire, then his shoulders start to relax a bit more after the fifth or sixth. That's my cue. I slide into the stool on his left, leaning forward and giving him an innocent smile. I make small talk and he starts to tell me about his issues with work and how he caught his wife cheating. I answer with an empathetic look and reassuring words as he knocks back a few more shots. When his head starts to sway and he looks at me in a bolder manner, it's time for my next move. I whisper in his ear and he nods, giving me a hungry look. He says to name the price. I raise it on Fridays, but that's okay with him. I hop into the passenger seat of his red Corvette and he takes us to his hotel.

The next morning, I wake up before him, slipping into the shower, and letting a few tears silently get washed away down the drain. That's the only place they ever go, down the drain. I didn't choose this life. They chose it for me. This is all I know. I dry off and slip back in beside him. Soon after, he wakes up, smiling down at me.

I trace the lines of his body and he leans over and kisses my cheek. I have once again achieved that look in his eye, like a craving that has finally been fulfilled. Then, leaving the bills rolled up and bound with elastic, he puts on his suit and tie and leaves.

REAPPROPRIATION

ASHLEY CALLINGBULL (CREE)
AND ANTHONY "THOSH" COLLINS (PIMA, SENECA-CAYUGA)

Model Ashley Callingbull and photographer Thosh Collins decided to "reappropriate" the fashion trend of wearing "Native" clothing. Ashley shares some of the authentic Native clothing that has been passed down in her family.

> The beadwork cuff was made by elders and passed on through my family. The beadwork moccasins I wear are twenty years old and were made by a Stoney woman.

Sixty-year-old moose-hide vest that belongs to my *mossum* (grandfather). He wore this while dancing traditional powwow.

Blanket by Pendleton.

My red fringe shawl was made by my great-great-grandmother.

Black vest circa 1952 made by my great-great-auntie Helen. Beadwork on cuff made by elders and passed down through my family.

Vintage 1960s western dress shirt and cowboy hat with eagle feather my *mossum* used to wear while dancing traditional powwow.

HEY, MR. GQ!

BUILDING MY OWN RUNWAY ON THE RESERVE

CHRISTIAN ALLAIRE

(Ojibway, Nipissing First Nation, and French-Italian)

Growing up as a weird fashion kid in northern Ontario—where I was even further segregated to the confines of the Nipissing First Nation reserve—I've definitely raised my share of eyebrows along the way. I've been that spectacle at family functions, the awkward boy wearing flashy shirts or jeans that are, now, admittedly, a little too tight. Even now when I make the journey from Toronto, where I work as a freelance fashion journalist, to Garden Village, the subdivision where most of my family resides, I still feel impending doom that my outfit will be scrutinized. "Hey, Mr. GQ!" says one of my cousins, always. "There's the city boy," says another. And it's not to say I don't bring it onto myself: spray-painted Dries Van Noten pants are probably a safer choice for the city streets.

First Nations communities, in all of their quirks and conventions, are much like any other small social groups: there exists a celebration of sameness. A celebration of ancestry, of traditions preserved,

I LONGED FOR THE FREEDOM TO EXPRESS MYSELF

and "the way things should be." While my cousins went hunting and four-wheeling, I was shopping for striped "arm warmers" and punk band tees, bands that I had never even listened to.

Once the punk phase proved passé, I went shockingly preppy in high school: American Eagle sweaters, designer jeans, striped polo shirts. My parents seemed to be supportive of this experimental

I SAW MY CULTURE, AND OTHER CULTURES, BEING STEREOTYPED AND OFTEN PLAGIARIZED

phase, but they did express their concern over the amount of time I was spending on my appearance.

I longed for the freedom to express myself, though, whether that was through spiked bracelets or weird formal suit vests. It never occurred to me that this obsession with fashion could later become a career, let alone one that I could achieve. My interests just felt weird at the time, like I was an extraterrestrial life form or an exchange student speaking another language. I even once asked my parents if I was adopted, preparing myself for the inevitable yes to follow.

Now, it's easy to see how my First Nations upbringing invoked this fire within me all along. When my sister got to co-design her first traditional dance regalia—a jingle dress that rocked the powwow—I remember admiring the detail and attention that was put into it. The chosen fabric colors all representing something personal,

the hours and hours of hand-sewing, the cut, the beading; if this didn't give me an appreciation for couture shows, what did?

This realization was further cemented when I moved away for school. After initially auditioning for several theater schools, none of which I was accepted into, I moved to Toronto to study journalism at Ryerson University. If I could not wear designer clothing like a movie star, I would write about it! There, I became transfixed by fashion journalism, thrusting myself into several fashion internships, including *Flare* magazine in Toronto and *Interview* magazine in New York. But arriving at my final destination (the fashion world) did not come without its faults.

The more I wrote and the more I styled, the more I began to notice the industry's increasing appropriation of my First Nations culture. Sure, it was there where I finally found people who speak my language, people who view clothing as wearable art (sometimes even masterpieces). But it was also where I saw my culture, and other cultures, being stereotyped and often plagiarized—and nobody else seemed to mind. Tribal patterns to the right! Headdresses to the left! Like some secret fashion super hero, I then decided: it would be up to me.

The integrity of my culture in fashion, and in general, is now something I constantly fight for—a strange twist of fate, given that fashion has always been the antithesis of what my community is all about. I remind myself of this now whenever I visit home. It doesn't matter if I don't fit within the typical confines of my culture, because my "weird" interests are actually bringing me closer to it. In fact, I admire it more than ever. I'm still a proud Native boy who loves coming home, even if that means breaking the mold from time to time.

Indian Giving

David Groulx (Ojibwe)

Canada gave the Indians religion
because it was cheaper
than giving them an education

Canada gave the Indians reserves
because it was cheaper
than killing them

Canada gave the Indians pails
because it was cheaper
than giving them clean water

Canada treats the Indians inhumane
because it believes
Indians are not human

Shapeshifter Gets a Job Offer

Courtney Powless (Mohawk)

Got a call from Enarcan
offering me big boy bucks
to dump nuclear waste
near Thunder Bay
and Elliot Lake. *Near Bisco*
too . . . at least there's no
documented harm.

Wish that Mohawk
would keep his mouth shut
about the toxic GM dump
in Akwesasne—*my sis says*
even the turtles have cancer
and diabetes from the PCBs
—and let me get on
with my business.

They may say
I'm a sellout.
I say, you gotta live
with one foot in each canoe.
Just eight more years
and I'm free
to be Anishinaabe.

SUPER INDIAN

COMIC BOOK BLUES

I SAVED THE REZ FROM A FOREST FIRE WITH MY *ICE BREATH* YESTERDAY.

What happens when an ordinary Native American 13-year-old boy eats commodity cheese* containing a food additive designed to enhance human strength, physicality, and endurance? He becomes Super Indian, the wacky web-comic and graphic novel series created, written, and illustrated by **Arigon Starr** (Kickapoo, Muscogee Creek, Cherokee, and Seneca).

Native super heroes aren't new. Natives have been featured in popular comics like *X-Men*, *Daredevil*, and *Turok* for decades. But in these comic books, Native artists and writers weren't behind the pencil. Arigon Starr and other comic artists in the Indigenous Narratives Collective are changing that by creating Native American super heroes drawn and written by Native American artists.

Q & A with Arigon Starr

How did you get started making graphic novels?

Native folks have always been doing "sequential art." You only have to take a look at pictographs—those are stories with pictures. *Super Indian* was originally a ten-part radio comedy series. Turning it into comic book form was always part of the plan!

What inspired you to create a Native American super hero?

Thinking about me and my sister as kids looking for something to read that had Native people in it. Anywhere. Even as a sidekick. I hope my work inspires other kids to write their stories, too.

Where do you get the ideas for the jokes in *Super Indian*?

In addition to my comics, I'm also a musician and actor, as well as a songwriter and playwright. Most people expect me to be an extrovert and do all the talking. However, I spend most of my time observing folks and listening. Real life is always much funnier than I could imagine.

Superman or Batman? Why?

Superman ... because he's a stranger in a strange land. Much like Native people are these days.

*Commodity cheese was processed cheese bought and stored by the government and given out to people in need from the 1960s to the 1990s.

"Like our languages, our stories hold the truth, our stories tell us who we are. It's time for us to tell OUR own stories OUR own way. Give me a mic—I'll share my stories, whether angry, silly, or offbeat—it's my truth that I'm trying to find—and I want to share that truth to give context to the past, present, and future. It's comedy, sure, but good comedy reflects life."

COMEDIAN RYAN MCMAHON ON LAUGHS AND LIFE

Funnyman Ryan McMahon (Anishinaabe) combines standup, improv, and sketch comedy in his irreverent, original comedy show, destroying stereotypes while getting laughs. @RMComedy#NDNCMDY

Poverty
FAITH TURNER
(Moose Cree First Nation)

Looking through the
mailbox slats

Today is that day

The brown envelope

Check has arrived

We will be okay for a whole
three days

Poverty is like running in one
spot and not getting anywhere

Can't get a job without
experience

Can't get experience
without a job

Standing there holding
her hand

We line up for a hot
bowl of soup

We line up to see our worker

We line up to receive our
paper bag of no-name cereal,
cabbage, and cans of beans
from the food bank

We line up to look through
the piles of clothing in the
donation bins

And maybe we can find
something nice to hang on
our wall in our small
apartment downtown

And Sally Ann will be
there Christmas morning
with a dolly for me

Trying to be a good quiet girl

It's Monday and there are
always so many offices to go to

I'm a big girl cause I'm five
years old and I can walk
fifteen blocks

The transfer ran out and we
are 50 cents short for bus fare

So much work to stay
at the bottom

Exhausted and tomorrow
we might have to do it all
over again

We learn to hand-wash
our clothes and hang them
everywhere to dry

Two dollars is important, it's a
loaf of bread or a bag of fries
for dinner

We use powdered milk and
what is Sugar Crisp? I get
puffed wheat from a bag
Add your own sugar

But the bannock is hot with
melted butter. It's our comfort
food

I realize now that we were
richer than we knew

Rich because we had
each other

Rich because we take in the
beauty of cloud-watching and
looking for four-leaf clovers

Our life so bright with color
because the festivals downtown
are free and they wear the
most beautiful costumes with
shiny ribbons, streamers,
and banners

Rich because we can spare
a few pennies to make
our biggest wishes in the
city fountain

Rich because the sun shines
on us and we have shade from
a tall tree at the park

Rich because climbing on the
jungle gym and sticking our
feet in the sand is free

Rich because there is a library
and it takes us away to places
of our imagination

Rich because we have a culture
so strong and rely on prayer

Rich because we appreciate
the music playing on the radio

Rich because we find any
luxury to be precious and
treasure it

Rich because no matter where
we go we remember where
we came from

We are rich mostly because we
find the strength in each other

Shedding my own *Skin*

Joseph Boyden
(Anishinaabe)

It was the best of times, it was the worst of times. I remember most clearly the sweet pain of falling in love, the exquisite anguish of wanting her to feel for me like I felt for her, and then the crushing weight of realizing she didn't and never would.

I remember being forced to attend an all-boys Catholic high school and failing my first class ever in grade nine and having to attend summer school. This was especially painful because I'd always been told that I was really smart, the top of my class. I no longer was. I was suddenly average. Less than average. This, possibly, is the moment I decided to rebel.

Here's something about me a lot of people don't know: I love reptiles and growing up raised all kinds of snakes in our basement: boa constrictors, a ball python, at one point a dozen rattlesnakes, and my most prized animal, Magnum, a Burmese python who, when I found him when I was just

I TRIED TO
END MY LIFE

eleven, was not even three feet long, and nine years later when I gave him to a zoo due to his sheer strength, an amazing thirteen feet of muscled grace.

I remember the girl I so desperately loved breaking up with me on my sixteenth birthday and me making the worst possible decision I could ever, ever make. I tried to end my life. I remember the weeks in hospital afterward, my many siblings coming to visit me with downcast eyes, not understanding why I would do something so horrible to them, why I would try so hard to hurt them. And this is exactly what I had done. It took years for me to realize that I had acted selfishly, so incredibly selfishly. But all that seemed to exist at the age of fifteen and sixteen were my pulsing, aching, confused emotions.

It took the rest of my teenage years to ultimately learn that to stop hurting so much inside, all I had to do was stop worrying about myself and try to help others who had less than me, who wanted to achieve their goals so badly but were being held back.

I remember becoming a tutor when I was asked to help the children of family friends who weren't succeeding in school. I recognized that when I shared my knowledge with them, they listened and understood and began to share their knowledge with me, too.

When I was seventeen, my former grade school asked me to bring my Burmese python, Magnum, in and show him to the students. He was ten feet long at this point, and they wanted me to talk about the strange and scary animal that wrapped himself around my neck and waist and chest and stared at the children with his slit eyes, his tongue darting out to taste their scent. I realized then, and when I began to bring my other reptiles to so many other local schools, that I was becoming a teacher, trying to explain to these kids with wide and fearful eyes that they didn't need to be so scared. And I remember the children slowly standing and nervously approaching to touch Magnum's thick, cool skin, how they commented that they thought for sure he was going to be slimy but he wasn't at all.

It's this, maybe, then, that allowed me to survive my teenage years. This growing realization that I had something worth sharing, that I could be bigger than my own anger and fear and sadness and that maybe, just maybe I had something others wanted a little bit of. I watched as my snakes shed their skin when they grew, the old peeling away and the new underneath so brilliantly new.

And I don't want to make it sound like everything was perfect after I began to

---

I GREW, SHEDDING OLD SKIN FOR SOMETHING BETTER

---

realize that I had something to give that others might want and need. That I was willing to share it because to help others when they need help is one of the most satisfying feelings there is. My teen years, when I think back on them now, were a roiling, boiling, incredibly intense time. They were sometimes amazing, and too often painful and brutal. But I grew, shedding old skin for something better, something that showed me I couldn't just survive in this world, but grow as supple and strong as I needed to be.

My teenage years were the most amazing years because these were the ones that, despite the setbacks showed me the promise and the beauty of the world and people around me. That time of my life proved that the more I reached out despite the fear of having my hand being bitten with sharp and needle python teeth, the more I began to see the world around me open up.

I remain a teacher, and I became a writer, because I always ultimately listened to what my gut told me. I still think of my python Magnum, and I hope he's happy and lazy, wrapped around the thick branch of a tree in some fancy zoo flicking his tongue and watching, knowing that the world spins all around him. But what I really hope is that Magnum was freed like I eventually became free and that he basks in the sunshine of Burma, his slit eyes smiling with the joy of life all around.

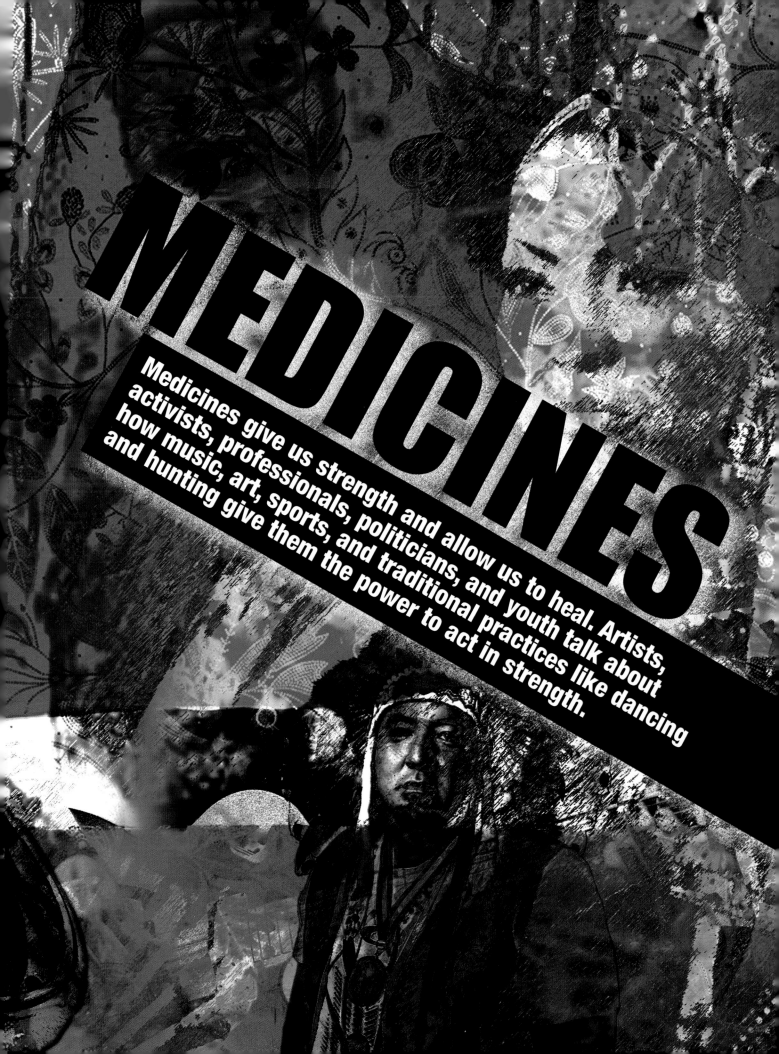

MEDICINES

Medicines give us strength and allow us to heal. Artists, activists, professionals, politicians, and youth talk about how music, art, sports, and traditional practices like dancing and hunting give them the power to act in strength.

MÉTIS VISUAL ARTIST
CHRISTI BELCOURT
SHARES THE SECRETS BEHIND HER EXTRAORDINARY PAINTING.

"THIS PAINTING IS AN ODE. I'M NOT A MUSICIAN SO IT'S MY SONG TO WATER."

WHAT INSPIRED THE PAINTING WATERSONG?

I was thinking about women, the importance of water, and the importance of preserving the most important resource that we have, which is our freshwater. The Great Lakes are being proposed as a route through which radioactive nuclear waste can be transported. There is a growing opposition to that idea. To me, there will probably come a day when human beings will realize that water is more precious than oil. We can live without oil, but we cannot survive without water.

WHAT IS YOUR PAINTING PROCESS LIKE?

I don't do full sketches of a painting. I will do sketches of particular plants if I need to understand them better. I paint the canvas black and then draw in with a light-colored pencil on top. The black background is inspired from the use of black trade cloth that historically was preferred for beadwork. The drawing process takes a lot of time. This painting took me four months to complete.

Watersong

WHAT ARE SOME OF THE DETAILS INCLUDED IN WATERSONG?

The roots in the painting show that there's more to life than what we see, in the spiritual sense. And also that our roots, our heritage, have great influence over our lives. Even if we're adopted, our ancestors are in us, and some of their memories are carried in our blood. The different species of plants that emerge from the same stem show that we are all connected in some way, shape, or form. The little brown, copperish reflective areas are the spirit world because there are spirits inside each plant, inside each living thing, inside the earth, and inside the universe.

WHY DID YOU INCLUDE THE OWLS?

Within some nations, it's believed that the spirit world will communicate with you through your dreams. They do that because in our waking life we are too busy thinking and following our own free will. Many times I'll get animals visiting me in my dreams, some enter repeatedly over time. I've learned to start listening to them. With the owl I was having several dreams over the period of a year, and when I painted her, she stopped coming into my dreams. I believe there are important lessons we can learn from other beings, and sometimes the spirits of these animals that communicate with us in our dreams are there to teach us things or to give us a message to carry to others.

WHAT'S THE STORY BEHIND THE SPIDERS?

When I was drawing onto the canvas, I noticed a little spider who had come and sat on the canvas, and I was drawing around it because I don't kill anything. It was there for about four days, and it finally dawned on me that the spider wanted to be in the painting. So I talked to the spider, apologized to it, and let it know that I would include it in the painting. I went downstairs to get tea, and when I came back the spider was gone. I placed four spiders in the painting, one for each day she sat waiting for me to clue in to her. I find this quite funny.

Why I Hunt

Hitting the reset button

JP Gladu
(Ojibwa, Sand Point First Nation)

From the time I could walk, I was around hunting. It was always about sustenance. My dad would tell me stories about when he was growing up. If they didn't snare or kill something, they didn't eat.

Hunting was the one reason I was allowed to skip school. If my dad ever caught my ass in an arcade or anything like that it would be blackened for weeks. As long as I was in the bush and my grades were good enough, I was allowed to occasionally be away from school.

Our reserve, the Sand Point First Nation, was taken away from us. In 1952, we were forcibly removed—houses torn down, the church and school were removed. They turned it into a provincial park. People from our community moved to neighboring reserves and all across Canada. Even to the United States. It wasn't until 2010 that we finally got our land back. So I grew up off reserve in Thunder Bay, very much integrated into mainstream society. Our parents did their best to make sure that we grew up connected to the land.

I left Thunder Bay when I was eighteen. I wanted to experience something else. I was always the oddball in my family. I have sixty-something first cousins, and I was the first person to graduate with a post-secondary education. I wanted a different adventure. I wanted to go to college and become a game warden.

Hunting is a reset button. When I'm working in my office in the city, it's a reminder of where I come from and why I do the things I do. When we do bring down a moose, I always cut the tip of the heart off and I'll find a birch tree and offer up a prayer to the Creator and leave my tobacco and thanks. I think that's why I'm successful every year. I respect the animal and I eat it. And I give it away to other people who eat it. I like sharing the stories because I don't think people really understand what it takes to go on the land and harvest an animal or some fish. I feel special that I can go and experience that year after year. It helps ground me and drives me to work harder.

I caught this rabbit on a winter snaring trip when I was nine. It was -40° Celsius (-40° Fahrenheit) the entire week but so memorable.

I was nineteen when I took this moose with my black Lab, Cody.

Bow hunting deer, Christmas 2012.

The Power of the Land

In every Nation, in every Clan
The Elders to a person,
Whether a woman or a man,
Shared a common truth,
One truth to understand,
That the spirit of the people
is equal
To the Power of the Land.
The mother of us all
The sacred Mother Earth,
Is constant in her giving,
And perpetual in her birth,
In meadows and in fields,
Where weeds and flowers grow,
She conceives the summer showers,
And spawns the winter snows.
In forests and in mountains,
She gives the birds that fly,
Every type of wing,
Then coaxes the wind to join,

In harmony when they begin to sing.
In brooks and streams,
And rivers as they flow,
She generates the dreams,
And makes the fires glow.
And in every creature,
Large and small,
She buries gems,
Of wisdom in them all,
And those that honor
Her creations
And acknowledge her grand design
Are given the templates
Of the sacred
And the patterns of the divine.
And then the certain knowledge,
This to understand
That the spirit of the people
is equal
To the Power of the Land.

Duke Redbird
(Ojibwa, Saugeen First Nation)

Music Is the Medicine

Singer-songwriter **Derek Miller** (Mohawk, Six Nations Reserve)

SOMEONE CALL AN ANGEL DOWN

I was reaching to the sky
Trying to pluck a star
I was hopeful for a while
But they're just a little too far

Round and round I go
Where I'll stop well I don't know
Maybe I should fly
Gently say good-bye

Someone call an angel down
It's getting too dark here on the ground
Someone call an angel down
It's getting too dark here on the ground

I was dreaming so regally
Lonesome on my trail
I was breathing in my life so deeply
And all the air was stale

Round and round we go
Where we stop I don't know
Maybe we should fly
Gently say good-bye

Someone call an angel down
It's getting too dark here on the ground
Someone call an angel down
It's getting too dark here on the ground

Maybe we should hold together
My dear crestfallen eyes
Tired as the hazy sun
Reachin' for disguise

Someone call an angel down
It's getting too dark here on the ground
Someone call an angel down
It's getting too dark here on the ground

I WROTE THIS SONG WHEN I WAS SEVENTEEN YEARS OLD.

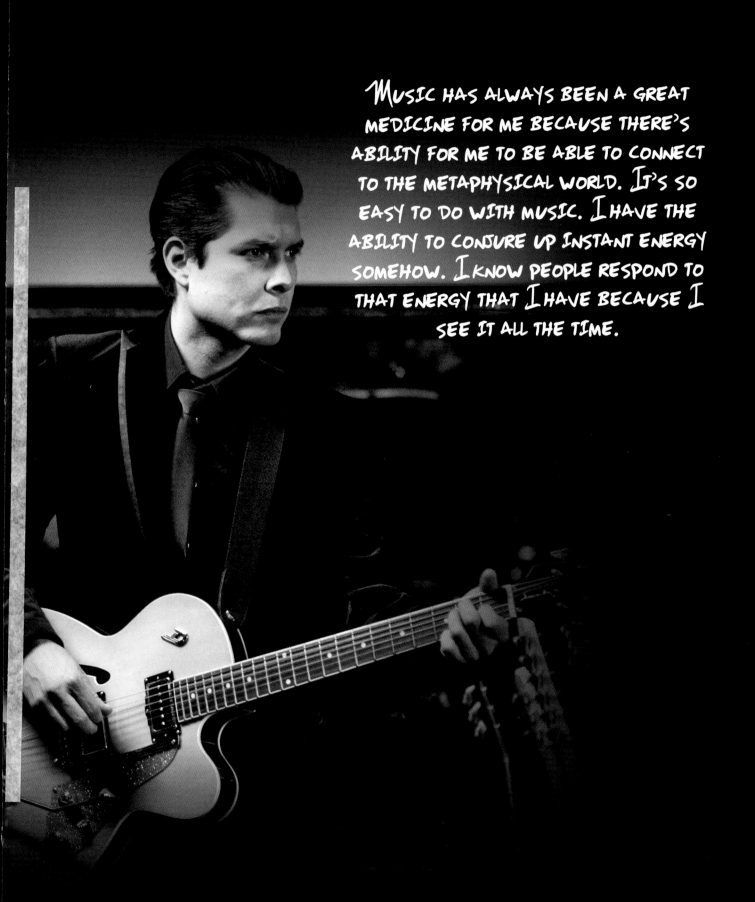

MUSIC HAS ALWAYS BEEN A GREAT MEDICINE FOR ME BECAUSE THERE'S ABILITY FOR ME TO BE ABLE TO CONNECT TO THE METAPHYSICAL WORLD. IT'S SO EASY TO DO WITH MUSIC. I HAVE THE ABILITY TO CONJURE UP INSTANT ENERGY SOMEHOW. I KNOW PEOPLE RESPOND TO THAT ENERGY THAT I HAVE BECAUSE I SEE IT ALL THE TIME.

Photograph by Nadya Kwandibens/Red Works Studio
(Anishinaabe, French, Northwest Angle # 37 First Nation)

OPENING MY EYES . . .
THE SUN DANCE CHANGED MY LIFE

CHAYLA DELORME MARACLE (CREE, MOHAWK) | PHOTOS BY CLAUDINE GLADUE (SADDLE LAKE CREE NATION)

I was thirteen and in grade eight when I started smoking weed. It wasn't something that came naturally. I forced myself to smoke it a few times to get used to it. I wanted to be able to smoke it around my Native friends. They weren't straight-A-type kids. They were associated with gangs. That's when I started drinking alcohol too. We'd drink it out of the bottle and get so drunk we blacked out. My mom didn't know what to do with me. She would try to hold on to me, and I would run away to go drink with my friends. The more aggressive she got in trying to stop me, the more it pushed me away. But I ended up being ganged up on by girls in the group. They beat me up so I quit hanging out with them.

It's funny but I started jingle dress dancing when I was around thirteen too. My mom kind of forced me to do it. It's not something I really wanted to do. I don't have any brothers

and sisters to help me within the powwow circle. I had to do it all by myself. I was so scared to dance at the powwows. I never did anything like that before. If I was smoking weed at the powwow, I would feel guilty for being high.

In grade nine I wasn't drinking a lot, but I was smoking a lot of weed. My high school life was more normal than my junior high though. I'd just hang out with my friends and drink and have fun and go to high school parties. In grade eleven, we started doing ecstasy. By grade twelve, we were doing it every weekend. I got a fake ID so I could go to clubs with my friends. By that point my mom and I had a trusting and honest relationship. She didn't overreact. She drove us to the club and picked us up to make sure we were safe. Toward the end of the year, it got really bad for me. My family was concerned because I wasn't happy. Even when I was doing the drug, it wasn't fun. It wasn't working for me anymore so I was taking more than I was supposed to be taking. If my mom wasn't there, it could have got worse and lots of bad things could have happened.

I quit drinking and doing drugs by myself two months after I turned eighteen. My mom had started going to Sun Dance. She told me that if I wanted to go I would have to be sober for a year to show my commitment. I wasn't ready to quit everything yet. Eventually,

I chose to quit because I wanted to share Sun Dance with her.

The Sun Dance was the most amazing experience. I'd always been involved in my culture since I was a child going to ceremonies such as sweats. But the Sun Dance really helped open my eyes to how strong Native culture and spirituality are . . . I'd never felt anything like that in my life. It's just a feeling

THERE'S A CONNECTION DIRECTLY BETWEEN YOU AND THE CREATOR AND THE DRUM

of pure happiness and pure love. Nothing—no drug—can compare to the feeling I felt at that Sun Dance. That's what helped me quit everything. I never wanted to drink or do drugs again because it would take away the connection that I have with Sun Dance.

Spirituality is not something you see, it's something you feel. When you're dancing, there's a connection directly between you and the Creator and the drum. It goes right to your heart, and it feels like you're so vulnerable and open. Some people say it's euphoria. Honestly, you have to experience it. It's amazing. Nothing else in my life has ever made me feel that way.

Spirituality is not something you see, it's something you feel.

The Sun Dance really helped open my eyes to how strong Native culture and spirituality are ... a feeling of pure happiness and pure love.

JINGLE DRESS DANCE IS A TRADITIONAL DANCE OF HEALING.

THE SUN DANCE IS THE MOST IMPORTANT RELIGIOUS CEREMONY OF THE PLAINS NATIONS.

CULTURE MATTERS

An interview with

Derek Nepinak

(Saulteaux),

Grand Chief of

the Assembly of

Manitoba Chiefs.

YOU HAVE AN IMPRESSIVE LIST OF ACCOMPLISHMENTS— ATHLETE, LAWYER, GRAND CHIEF. WHAT ARE YOU MOST PROUD OF? WHY?

I'm most proud of being a dad. I do my best at the most difficult job of parenting. That is, being an effective parent is not easy, no matter what your other accomplishments in life might be. I don't feel pride generally in the roles people put me in. I'm honored to have experienced a lot of different things in life, each demanding my best effort in one way or another. My kids challenge me every day though, and they make me proud every day.

YOU HELPED DESIGN A PROGRAM FOR ABORIGINAL YOUTH THAT PROMOTED CULTURAL AWARENESS. WHY DID YOU THINK YOUTH SHOULD HAVE THAT EXPERIENCE?

I knew that if young people had an opportunity to learn their culture and be exposed to positive cultural outlets, they would have a better chance of developing positive identity markers and increase their chances of reaching goals later in life. A solid identity built by positive exposure to culture is critically important for our people, particularly with embedded and systemic racism throughout many of the public institutions that we deal with every day. The racism throughout Canada is very subtle in some instances, and many people succumb to its negative energy by becoming angry. Oftentimes people don't even know why they became angry. With a solid identity built from positive exposure to who we are, we can overcome and transcend those things that would otherwise hold us down.

WHAT ADVICE DO YOU HAVE FOR THE ABORIGINAL YOUTH READING THIS BOOK?

Pay attention to your elders, stay focused on getting education, and set personal goals for achievement. If a person is able to establish themselves on a personal platform of the seven teachings, then they are on their way to a good life. It's not easy though. It takes great commitment, and oftentimes people sway off course in complex and challenging times. It's important during those times to be able to forgive yourself. This requires a lot of self-respect and humility.

HOW DO ABORIGINAL YOUTH INSPIRE YOU?

There is nothing more passionate than our youth. Their hearts contain the purest forms of raw passion that can change the world! We all saw this during Idle No More. Sometimes people say that Idle No More rallies didn't do anything. Truth is, to me, the youth inspired a generation of our people to stand strong and make a difference. The effects of Idle No More and the youth movement will not be entirely felt for years to come.

A GRAND CHIEF IS ELECTED TO LEAD A COUNCIL OF CHIEFS.

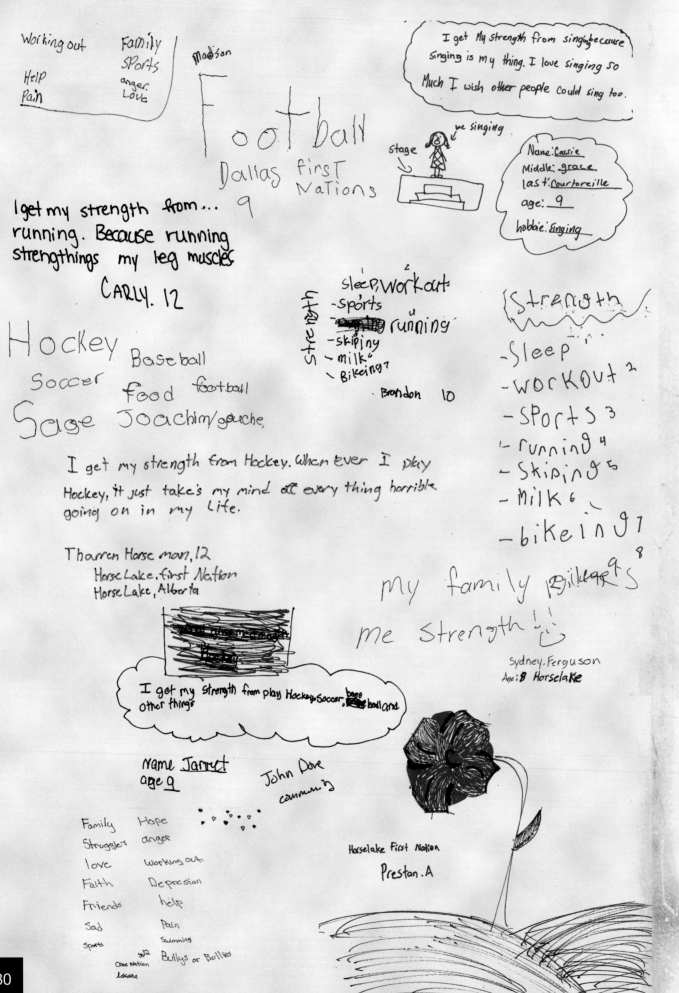

Working out   Family
                Sports
Help   anger
Pain   LOVE

Madison

I get My strength from singing because singing is my thing. I love singing so Much I wish other people Could sing too.

F o o t b a l l
Dallas First Nations
9

stage   me singing

Name: Cassie
Middle: grace
Last: courtoreille
age: 9

hobbie: singing

I get my strength from...
running. Because running
strengthings my leg muscles
CARLY. 12

Hockey   Baseball
  Soccer   football
        Food
Sage Joachim/gauche

I get my strength from Hockey. When ever I play Hockey, it just take's my mind off every thing horrible going on in my Life.

Tharren Horse man, 12
  Horse Lake. First Nation
  Horse Lake, Alberta

I get my Strength from play Hockey, Soccer, base ball and other things

Name Jarret
age 9

John Dove
community

Family   Hope
Struggles   anger
love   Working out
Faith   Depresion
Friends   help
Sad   Pain
Sports   Swimming
           Bullys or Bollies
Cree Nation
Loretta

strength
Sleep, workout
- sports
- running
- skiping
- milk
- Bikeing
Brandon 10

Strength

-Sleep
-workout 2
-sports 3
-running 4
-skiping 5
-Milk 6
-bikeing 7

my family gives me Strength !!!

Sydney. Ferguson
Age: 8 Horselake

Horselake First Nation
Prestan. A

Kaden Horseman

I am strong when I have to leave my dad and go back to to my mom in coldlake because iam alone there.

name Kaden Horsemen

age iam ten years old
nationHorselake firstnation

Coldlake, Grandprairie,
Kelley lake, Horselake

I get My Strength from the other people around the Rez by knowing they didn't go to school and now they can't get good Jobs. so I look at them and I don't want to be like that. So I am focused on school and in 2 more years I graduate. and I play a lot of sports like rugby, Football, Hockey, basketball, baseball, and golf, to Keep from doing drugs and other things.

Nuveda Mhii 16

I get my strength from my family supporting me. I alsa get it from my passion for sports help

me to try and go beyond my limits.

I alsa get it from my Sick flow.

Prestan
8yrs
Horselake first Natron

WHAT GIVES YOU STRENGTH?
YOUTH SHARE THEIR ANSWERS
from Horse Lake First Nation, Alberta

Sokolum
on the Small Screen

I'm Heather Hill a.k.a. Sokolum from Yellowknives Déné First Nation in the Northwest Territories. I now live in Montreal. I was an auditor with the government for four years, and I found it to be too repetitive so I decided to change careers. My natural choice was my favorite hobby: makeup!

In 2008, I started creating my YouTube beauty tutorials for fun and to interact with others about makeup. I didn't expect people to enjoy them as much as they have. I get recognized every once in a while, mostly when in a makeup store. People will either come up to me to say hi or I will get a message on Instagram or YouTube saying that they saw me. It's always very flattering to talk to people who "know" me and enjoy my extreme looks.

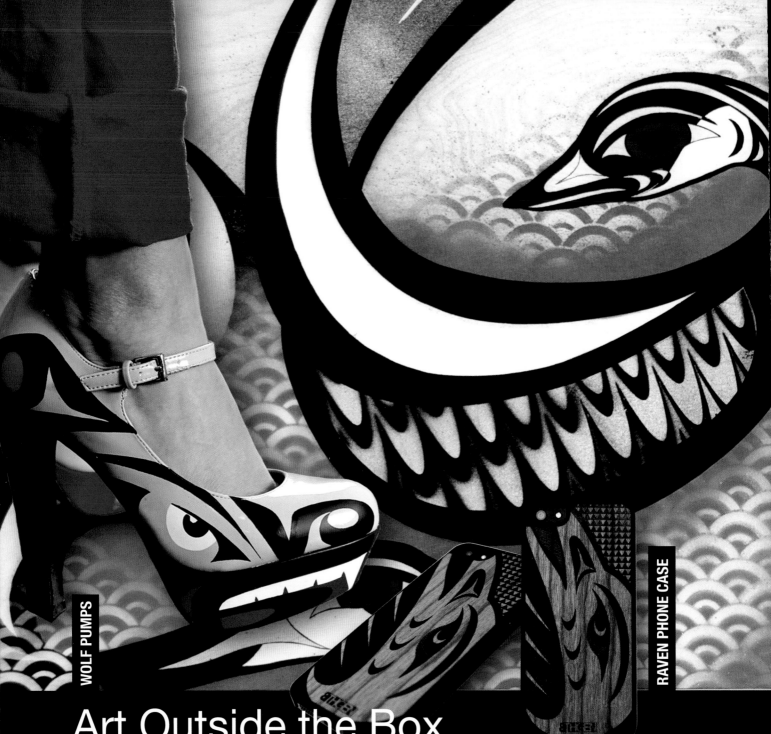

WOLF PUMPS

RAVEN PHONE CASE

Art Outside the Box

Artist and activist **Louie Gong** *(Nooksack) merges traditional Coast Salish art with everyday pop culture objects to create unique, accessible art with a rich message about mixed-race heritage.*

Louie Gong grew up in Ruskin, British Columbia, and the Nooksack tribal community in Washington State with his grandparents, father, and stepmom. He is of Nooksack, Squamish, Chinese, French, and Scottish heritage.

When Louie was working as an education resource coordinator for Muckleshoot Tribal College, he decided to buy a pair of Vans—shoes that he had wanted when he was a kid but couldn't afford. Since he couldn't find any patterned styles that he liked, he bought a gray pair. After helping to paint traditional designs on hand drums one day at work, he came home, grabbed a marker, and started drawing traditional Northwest Salish images on

TRIANGULATE PAINTING

TREE FROG VANS

HUNT AND PREY HIGHTOPS

the Vans. Louie wore them to work the next day and was soon taking orders to customize shoes for other people.

His art business grew from there. Now the self-taught artist and entrepreneur's company, Eighth Generation, produces original artwork in the form of shoes, skateboards, prints, and more.

Louie uses his art and his time to raise awareness about racial and cultural identity. As an internationally recognized leader on this issue, he travels around the world speaking and leading workshops to help foster a deeper understanding of the challenges and rich gifts of being multiracial.

"I work on projects that are values-driven and enjoyable. If you put your heart into tasks that have those characteristics, you can accomplish what most people can't even imagine possible."

"Health and fitness is something I'm passionate about. It's the fundamental building block of any nation."

HOW DID YOU GET INVOLVED IN SPORTS?

My mother was a well-known Native rights activist. She expected my sisters and I to do our best. She encouraged us to push ourselves physically and academically. She knew we'd be up against a lot of stereotypes. She wanted us to be fit. She got us into sports at a really young age. She knew that the perseverance it taught us was an important building block for life. She'd tell us, "Do your best. I'll be there with you. I'll give you the tools. Don't disrespect yourself by being lazy, by giving up."

The Power of Sport

An interview with
WANEEK HORN-MILLER (Mohawk)
FORMER OLYMPIAN AND HEALTH AND WELLNESS ADVOCATE

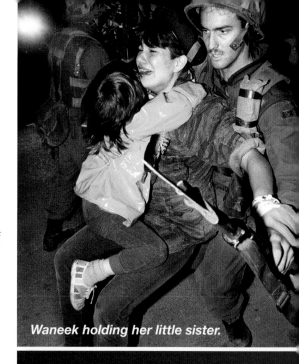

Waneek holding her little sister.

WHEN YOU WERE JUST 14 YEARS OLD, YOU WERE INJURED ON THE FRONT LINES OF THE OKA CRISIS. HOW DID THAT AFFECT YOU?

Oka was an eye-opening experience for everyone. It put Native issues on the front page of newspapers. Many people realized they weren't taught the real history of Canada. I saw a lot of awful racism. And, I saw my community showing a lot of pride. I suffered a lot of post-traumatic stress after I was stabbed by a Canadian soldier's bayonet. I used sport to help. I was a good athlete. I'd already been the Ontario provincial champion in swimming and the city champion in running. My dream of going to the Olympics started long before the Oka crisis.

WHY IS INDIGENOUS HEALTH SO IMPORTANT TO YOU?

Health and fitness is something I'm passionate about. It's the fundamental building block of any nation. And, it's the number one issue in the Aboriginal community. I host a TV show called *Working It Out Together*. It's about improving fitness and wellness in the Aboriginal community. I wanted to provide people with some resources that I've had —doctors, nutritionists, and personal trainers—that they could benefit from. I realized that getting fit and staying well is more complicated for some people. You need to figure out what stops people from becoming fit. It made me think about where I would be if I didn't have the goal of competing in the Olympics and the support of my family.

IN 2000, YOU COMPETED AT THE SYDNEY OLYMPICS AS THE CO-CAPTAIN OF THE CANADIAN WOMEN'S WATER POLO TEAM. WAS IT DIFFICULT BEING THE ONLY ABORIGINAL ATHLETE ON THE OLYMPIC TEAM?

Yes, of course. Canadian Olympic teams are still not very reflective of the people of the nation. Generally they're made up of white, middle-to-upper-class people. The cost involved in pursuing a sport means it's not accessible to many. I had a hard time with the hierarchical nature of sports. But I still wanted to pursue my dream. The sports world used my differences, like putting me on the cover of *TIME* magazine with an eagle feather in my hair. But it wasn't interested in what I brought in terms of my Aboriginal perspective.

WHAT HAVE YOUR EXPERIENCES TAUGHT YOU?

Many Canadians see Aboriginal people as a burden, with nothing to contribute to the mainstream. This is not true. We have an increasingly large amount of knowledge, culture, and strength that non-Aboriginal Canadians could greatly learn from. The most important thing that I learned on this journey is that if we can figure out a way to get along, to respect our differences, we can accomplish a lot. You have to find a common ground.

THE OKA CRISIS

In the summer of 1990, Oka, a small town in Quebec, Canada, started to develop a golf course and luxury condos on ancestral burial grounds of the Mohawk community of Kanesatake. Since the eighteenth century the Mohawks had been unsuccessful in their attempts to press the government to recognize their right to land in the area. This time, the Mohawks protested by setting up barricades to the development site. The police were called in and the standoff became violent. The conflict over Native land claims became front-page news, and the Mohawks were joined by Natives from across Canada and the United States. The RCMP and the Canadian army were called in. After seventy-eight days, the Mohawks put down their weapons and ended the standoff. In 1997, the federal government purchased the land from Oka and the Mohawks were allowed to expand their existing cemetery, but have not been granted their right to the land.

In his paintings, Bunky Echo-Hawk (Pawnee and Yakama) combines traditional images and pop culture references, using humor to draw attention to issues facing Native American communities. A committed activist and educator, Echo-Hawk travels around the United States holding art events to raise money for nonprofit organizations. He creates his large-scale paintings live in front of an audience and then auctions them off.

Modern Warrior

PAINTER AND HIP HOP ARTIST BUNKY ECHO-HAWK USES HIS ART TO FIGHT FOR CHANGE

"There is a lot of ignorance, pre-conceived notions about who we are, a lot of misconceptions, a lot of stereotypes. I feel through art I can attack some of these."

"There are a great number of issues facing Native Americans today, which I confront with my choice of weapons: paints, brushes, canvas, my mind, and my culture."

89

DREAMCATCHERS

Through art and activism, education and entrepreneurship, Indigenous people across North America turn their dreams into realities.

Life Lessons

Model **Jade Willoughby** (Ojibway and Jamaican) shares her surprising story.

When **Jade Willoughby** from Whitesand First Nation was growing up in Thunder Bay, Ontario, she suffered from a kidney disease called Nephrotic syndrome. From the age of seven to sixteen, when she finally went into remission, her disease made her look obese and she was ridiculed by other kids.

Learning to deal with rejection and being rooted in culture (she's a jingle dress powwow dancer) have helped the two-spirited young woman to become more determined in her modeling career and continue to strive for success in a tough industry.

MY STORY

I lived like the bubble boy often.

I was essentially in a little quarantine.

I couldn't interact with people other than those who lived in my household. I was homeschooled, so needless to say I didn't necessarily have the best social skills in the world.

When I could go back to school, having the physical appearance that I did, it was very, very difficult. Kids would call me chipmunk cheeks.

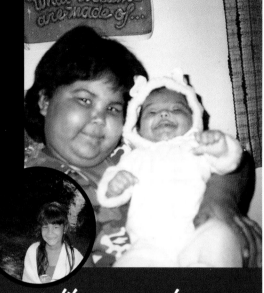

I have my moments like anyone else where I break down. I've had my days where I say I don't want to do this anymore, its too hard, I'm lonely, I want to go home, I want to stop. Anytime it gets too hard, I remember the people in my life that I've lost because they had things that were too hard, that were hard for them.

I've lost, very recently, several of my family members to suicide. I draw on the memories of my loved ones and think, I have to do it.

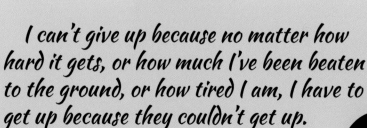

I can't give up because no matter how hard it gets, or how much I've been beaten to the ground, or how tired I am, I have to get up because they couldn't get up.

-JADE

94

Each year the Edd sisters travel to the Santa Fe Indian Market, the world's largest Native American arts show.

Adventure in Art

Ruthie, Sierra, Chamisa, and Santana Edd
(Diné Nation) share a family—and a love of art.

I go to Fort Lewis College, double majoring in Native American and Indigenous Studies and World History, with a minor in Biology. I go to class, have a job, participate in club activities, and try to stay active. Wherever I can, I try to incorporate art, whether that be doodling in my notes, sketching while listening to an audiobook, or just looking at artwork others have done. I'm inspired by Native artists like Shonto Begay and Frank Buffalo Hyde, and non-Native artists like Frida Kahlo and Michelangelo.
— **Ruthie**

My art references important issues in Native American history in a contemporary modern art style. I'm grateful when people ask questions about my art and want to learn more. My main purpose with my art is to educate non-Native Americans to be aware of issues that affect Native American society. I also like to write poetry and stories. I tend to base my poetry on Native American culture. I have started a graphic novel about contemporary Native life, using humor to address some important social realities.
— **Sierra**

My art is inspired by Navajo culture. My paintings show how things are today or are tales of Navajo myths. The best thing about showing my art at the Indian Market is the feedback I get from the judges and the people shopping. Their advice helps me to strive to make better art. When I'm not making art, I usually hang out with my sisters, walking downtown and stopping by a candy shop. I also play games like Rock, Paper, Scissors, the DS, basketball, and lacrosse.
— **Chamisa**

Some of the subjects I paint are a combination of realistic and abstract, because I like the way it looks. I care a lot about the texture in my artwork. It has to match the painting's feelings. If I'm painting a face with a tear, I try to make it look real. When I'm not working on art I try to spend time with my family, but it can be hard because everybody has a busy schedule. I like to read graphic novels, chapter books, and once in a while some picture books.
— **Santana**

Reunited

Sharai Mustatia | Métis, Cree, French

I stood in the doorway of the kitchen feeling awkward and out of place.

"Do ya want some coffee?" Celia offered from the other end of the kitchen.

"Uh, no thanks, I think we wanna go out, is that okay?" I was feeling timid. I didn't want to stutter so I poured the words from my mouth like molasses.

My friend Veronica chimed in, "We're thinking of going out for lunch, the three of us."

I knew that Celia didn't want Kimi to be alone with me. Maybe she asked Veronica to be a chaperone. I had no idea and it wouldn't surprise me if she did. I just wanted to be with my daughter.

Kimi started to tidy up her untouched plate of pancakes.

Celia's voice sounded a bit shaky. "It's okay, you should just go, I'll clean up."

I stood near the stairwell of the main entrance, on the stained beige carpet. I tried to not look around but couldn't help it. I saw pictures of their family. Pictures of Kimi through the years, starting from the day they brought her home. There they were forever captured together. Posed. Connected. Family. All the things I missed out on in her growing up. The first day of school. The first picture she would draw to bring home for me to hang on the fridge. I missed it all.

Together me, Kimi, and Veronica left the house. It was a relief to get out into the fresh air again. To not feel stifled by the tension I sensed inside. They were only letting Kimi meet me because she'd been asking for a few years and wouldn't let the issue go.

"A few years?" I'm impressed by Kimi. Her agency. Her independent thinking. I want to believe that genetically, she gets her sense of justice from me.

We're in the mall in the south end of town at the Smitty's restaurant. It smells like cheap coffee and burgers frying. The sound of dishes clanging together is making me jumpy. I can hear an old lady hacking up a lung just after she lights her cigarette. I'm sitting across the booth from Kimi so I can have a clear view of her. Veronica is sitting beside her, sideways, with her leg bent and pulled up onto the sticky vinyl seat.

"You can order anything you want, Kimi." I know she's hungry because we interrupted her brunch.

"Um, okay, I'm not really hungry." She's twiddling her fingers nervously.

"Please order something, we're going to be out for the afternoon and you'll get hungry."

I'm staring at Kimi like she's a work of art. She's so beautiful. I want to push her back inside me. I want to try again. But this time I won't give her up so easily or even at all. To turn back the clock and be pregnant again. To deliver her again. To hold her at my breast, in my arms again. To never let her go ever.

There are lulls in conversation as I try to find my words. I don't feel interesting and forget my preplanned questions. The kid in

Artwork by **Kristina Bad Hand** *(Sicangu Lakota and Cherokee)*

the next booth is trying to play peek-a-boo with us; we don't want to join in but do, unenthusiastically, anyway.

"How's school? What grade are you in?" I say in between peek-a-boos, with a mouth full of French fries.

"Not bad," Kimi replies.

Throughout the conversation she mostly says, "I dunno. Maybe. I guess." Kids her age don't have much to say to adults, let alone their birth mothers who give them up for adoption. Maybe she wants to talk to me but doesn't know how. The feeling is mutual.

We finish up our burgers and I can feel the coffee jitters setting in. My hands are visibly shaking. I walk beside Kimi and try to get a whiff of her. What I really want to do is grab her and put her in my lap and sniff her head and body like I did when she was mine.

"What should we do?" I ask Veronica and Kimi.

"Let's go to Walmart and you guys should get portraits!" Veronica suggests.

I'm not sure about the idea. I'm not sure if Kimi will want to do that.

"Come on, you guys! When's the next time you're gonna see each other? This'll be something for you to always remember this day."

As though I would, or could, ever forget. We walk through the mall to the other end where the Walmart is. I am anxious about getting pictures because my face is so blotchy and red from all the nervous sweating I am doing. I use the sleeve of my navy blue, itchy, cheap wool sweater to wipe my face, which makes my face redder. Veronica walks directly up to the portrait area where there is a woman working.

"We need to get portraits of these two together." She's pointing with her thumb back at Kimi and me standing behind her.

I look at Kimi to try to get a feeling of what she's thinking. Like I can read her mind. But I can't even read her face.

"I'm sorry, we're all booked today," the photographer says to Veronica, who is practically sitting on top of the portrait counter now.

"Oh well, it's okay." I start to walk away, Kimi beside me.

"Really? You can't fit them in anywhere today?" Veronica is getting aggravated.

"No I'm sorry, there are two people ahead of you and then I have to close. You can come back first thing tomorrow."

Veronica pauses for a moment and says, "Look, these two've just been reunited. Lizzie gave Kimi up for adoption and this is the first time they've seen each other since Kimi was a baby."

"Veronica, no, it's okay." My face is burning raw from the intense heat that's building in my body.

"They don't know when they'll see each other again." Veronica has her "I mean business" voice on.

"Oh, oh my god! Okay, I can squeeze you in before I close tonight. Come back at five and we'll do it then."

"Good." Satisfied with herself for making things happen, Veronica looks at me and says, "Let's go wander."

I feel stunned. I don't have the money to pay for portraits. We wander around looking at things, making awkward conversation. Kimi doesn't like me. She thinks I'm boring.

"What's your favorite color?" I ask Kimi, who's eyeing the paper and pens lining the aisle. I watch her fingertips lightly caress the expensive handmade paper. We both love paper and pens. I like that we have that in common.

She tells me but I don't hear her. I'm hypnotized, enamored, fascinated, and in awe of this young girl who is my daughter, standing there beside me looking at pens.

"I'm a writer," Kimi tells me as a matter of fact.

"That's awesome! What do you write?"

"I'm writing an epic. A series. It's going to be at least six books."

"Wow! That's a big job!" I believe her.

I ask her questions about her epic and she tries, "It's sort of a fantasy type thing."

"Oh yeah, what about? Like, is it an adventure thing like Dungeons and Dragons?"

"Kind of. I'm still developing the characters."

She is so serious. Short sentences and deliberate answers. Doesn't leave much room for getting to know her. But what is my hurry? I guess I'm just so afraid of how quickly things can change and how quickly people leave our lives. When my dad committed suicide, I learned just how bad it felt to regret not telling someone how you felt. I never want to regret not saying everything I had to say to someone I love, ever again.

THE ROAD TO THE RED CARPET

Award-winning actress **Michelle Thrush** (Cree) on her dramatic journey.

Michelle and co-star Benicio del Toro at the Cannes Film Festival

Every time I would see a Native person on TV I just felt a connection as a kid—and so much pride. I didn't think acting would be a career. I just thought it was something you did for fun. I wanted to be a social worker or go into political science. And then I met Native actor Gordon Tootoosis, and he really gave me a lot of encouragement to get into acting. He encouraged me to move out to Vancouver when I was nineteen.

I was really determined—I started auditioning and didn't get many roles when I was younger. There wasn't much happening with Native actors. I was waitressing and doing everything else that I needed to pay my bills.

It's really important if you want to be in the arts to come from a place of wanting to tell stories, from a real and honest place. If you come from that place, nothing is going to stop you; no amount of rejection is going to stop you from wanting to tell your story.

We come from an oral tradition, and we know that storytelling is a big part of who we are. I do arts workshops with children and youth. The beauty of using theater is that you are not preaching to people—you are using emotions. You are allowing people to identify and to feel on a level that they aren't being dictated to, they are being brought along on that journey. When you're on that journey, I always tell youth to trust what they are feeling. Trusting your feelings is the first step in healing.

When I was a kid, I thought I was the only person in the whole world who was living in a home that was so messed up. I try really hard to allow kids to see the fact that I grew up in a really difficult situation, but I used the arts to transform that into something that was working for me. It's a very powerful transformation.

TIPS FROM THE MUSICAL TRENCHES

Award-winning Métis musician **Conlin Delbaere-Sawchuk**, part of the Métis Fiddler Quartet, offers advice to aspiring musicians.

WORK TOWARD ACHIEVABLE GOALS

If you're passionate about music and working on it, I can't emphasize how important it is to have a good plan. Talent and abilities take time to nurture and you've always got to give yourself objectives that you can achieve, otherwise you'll be discouraged and won't want to achieve your dreams.

CHALLENGE YOURSELF

Set objectives, like learning a scale or listening to a song, and learn it in your head and then learn to play it—learn the chords that go with that melody, and then you can learn to play it. If you start by learning something small and basic, then you can start to combine things. If you learn things in steps, then you progress.

BE AN ARTIST AND AN ENTREPRENEUR

Although a postsecondary education in music can help to hone skills and abilities as an artist, it is important to have a career goal in mind. And, whatever your goals, it's important to find a balance between artistic satisfaction and commercial success. As I pursued my degree in music, I realized that learning to manage the business end of my career and pursuing performance opportunities were important to me. Sometimes, this led me to take time off from school to play shows, which annoyed some of my professors but helped me to build my career.

KEEP YOUR MIND OPEN TO OPPORTUNITIES

Everyone has a dream, and it's always worth pursuing your dreams, but don't get hung up on them. Keep an open mind, and let your dreams evolve.

LET'S JOIN HANDS

IDLE
NO
MORE

AND TAKE A STAND

To me, the Idle No More movement is about recognizing the need for change. By joining hands and taking a stand, we will support one another along this journey. With strength and persistence, we will succeed in creating a better world for ourselves and for future generations.
—Kelli Clifton (Tsimshian)

Idle No More!

Say No to Oil Shale and Tar Sands Mining.

PROTECT OUR FUTURE

Utah State Capital

Los Angeles, California

-C-45
...S MORE
...I MY
...PER!!!

IF YOU DRINK WATER, YO ARE AFFECTED BY RTI .L C-45

Tk'emlups to Secwepemc, British Columbia

Times Square, New York City

THE IDLE NO MORE MOVEMENT BEGAN IN DECEMBER 2012 AS A CALL FOR PEOPLE TO JOIN A PEACEFUL REVOLUTION TO HONOR INDIGENOUS SOVEREIGNTY AND TO PROTECT THE LAND AND WATER. POWERED BY SOCIAL MEDIA, TEACH-INS, PROTESTS, ART SHOWS, AND OTHER EVENTS, THE MOVEMENT TOOK PLACE ACROSS NORTH AMERICA.

ILL STAND FOR MY

York Factory Band, Manitoba

Flash Mob Grand Entry, West Edmonton Mall, Alberta

103

In all honesty, it wasn't a matter of having a choice of whether or not to participate in Idle No More, it was all around me. It was on every social network, it was on the television, my friends talked about it, my classes had discussions, and much of my family went to rallies. During the peak of the Idle No More movement, there wasn't a day that went by that there wasn't something new to hear or something new to learn, and I continue to learn more each day.

Aaron Paquette, the speaker at the Edmonton Idle No More rally, said you are a spark that ignites a thousand more people. I believe in what he said. Although I am a youth and my efforts and my voice may seem small, it doesn't change the fact that my voice influences my younger siblings, my friends, and my family. My participation in Idle No More makes a difference because every time I speak about the Indigenous struggles, it is one more person who is willing to help our battle.

I participate in INM every day by changing the way I live my life and the way I think about the world. Every time I read a book, an article, a newspaper, or watch a video in an effort to learn more about my culture, I am participating. Every time I contact new people asking for their guidance on how to learn more about my heritage, I am participating. In my opinion, to be idle no more the people must let go of the materialistic society's way of thinking and learn to think and live the way our ancestors once did.

—**Raquel Simard** (Manigotagan Métis and Oji-Cree First Nation)

Westlake Mall, Burbank, California

Los Angeles, California

West Edmonton Mall, Alberta

medicine war love

Kris Statnyk (Vuntut Gwitchin Youth)

witiko lover
heart as cold as ice

the winter in our bed
is here to stay

make way make treaty
—surrender

make medicine
war love

a ceremony
to keep in the dark

inside a cold
government house

under wood smoke
& gifted blankets

—we will burn it all
return it in the end

it always comes back
stronger in the end

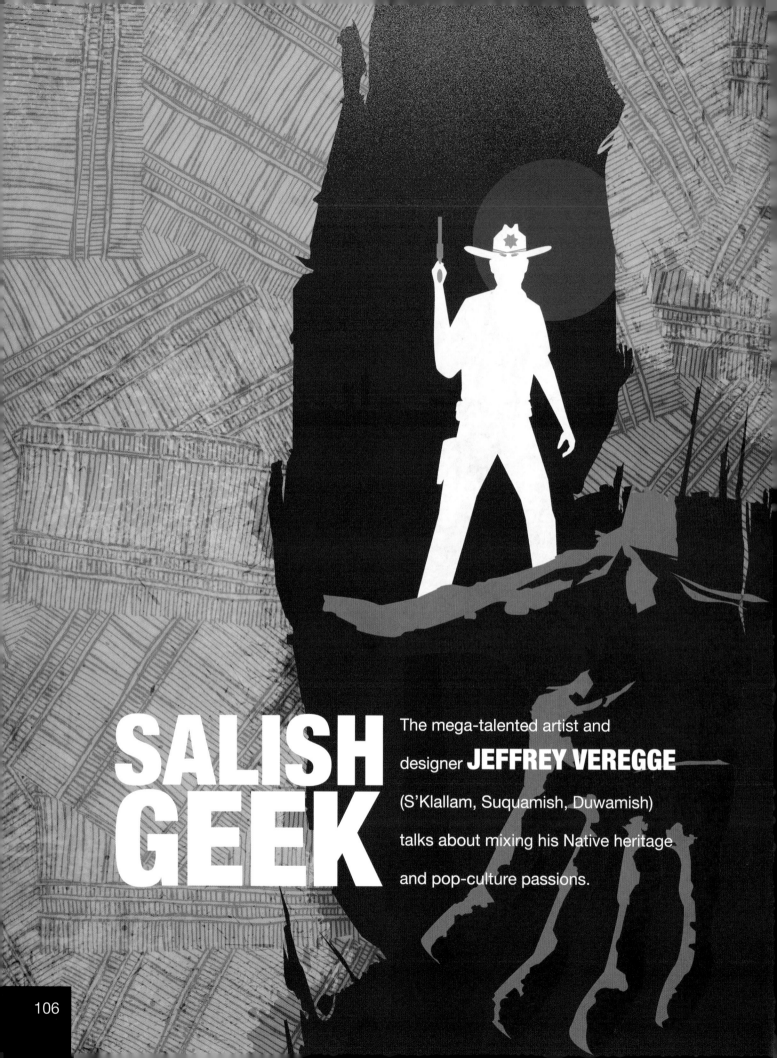

SALISH GEEK

The mega-talented artist and designer **JEFFREY VEREGGE** (S'Klallam, Suquamish, Duwamish) talks about mixing his Native heritage and pop-culture passions.

I CALL MYSELF AN INDIAN NERD OR SALISH GEEK. I AM NOT JUST ONE OR THE OTHER. I AM BOTH EQUALLY AND I AM GOOD WITH THAT.

WHAT ARTISTS INFLUENCED YOU GROWING UP?

In my own tribe, I was exposed to art. Jake Jones and Joe Ives are great artists—both master carvers and painters who have created quite a visual legacy among our people. But as a kid it was always the printed ink of the comics and the movies that made me the most excited. George Lucas, Steven Spielberg, Ray Harryhausen, and Walt Disney were all like great-uncles that I wished I could hang around with. Their influence can be seen very much in what I create today.

Jeffrey and his mom

WHAT WAS YOUR CHILDHOOD LIKE?

I was raised in Kingston, Washington, on the Port Gamble S'Klallam Reservation known locally as Little Boston. My rez is not a big one, but we are right on the water. Almost my entire family on my mom's side is there. Growing up with all my cousins close by, being able to go to any of my aunts' and uncles' homes, always feeling loved and welcomed, are great memories I cling to. One of my favorite things was to listen to my mom and aunties' gossip sessions. They would be funny, colorful, and gave me more laughs than I can remember anywhere else as a child.

Besides my aunties' homes, two other places on my rez had a huge effect on who I am today: the community church and the Tribal Public Library. I loved both for separate reasons. The church on our rez at the time was an old drafty building. Although it was freezing most of the time, it could be the warmest place on all the rez. It was here I was first exposed to God, Jesus, and the Bible, and although my language is a bit salty, my humor a bit twisted, all are still an important part of my life today.

The other place that I loved going was the library. Here I could get lost for hours looking at all the books on dinosaurs, astronomy, movies, mythology, and arts and crafts. My favorites were these monster books, the Crestwood House Monster Series! Here I could stare at images of Godzilla, Frankenstein, Dracula, the Mummy, King Kong, and never get bored or tired. Like a drug, it left me wanting more. When the library started adding movies that you could check out, it was like getting your meal supersized for free. I know I would not be the same artist had it not been for that library.

ON YOUR WEBSITE, YOU HAVE THIS QUOTE FROM BRUCE WAYNE IN *BATMAN BEGINS*: "IT'S NOT WHO I AM UNDERNEATH, BUT WHAT I DO THAT DEFINES ME." WHY?

For me, this is more than just quoting one of my favorite characters. To me, it is telling the world, you may see me as one thing. But my actions will tell you who I really am.

Much like my Vulcan hero, Spock, I am of mixed heritage. My mom is Native (S'Klallam, Suquamish, and Duwamish) and my dad is French/German. At times, it felt like each world had an opinion of what this meant for me. There have been moments where I struggled with this myself. As an artist, I wasn't sure where I could go. I appreciated what both worlds had to offer but never felt like I could choose just one.

The work you see today is years of internal battles, cultures waging war on my heart being brought together by a common interest of just being me. That is why I call myself an Indian Nerd or Salish Geek. I am not just one or the other. I am both equally and I am good with that.

IF YOU COULD GIVE YOUR YOUNGER SELF ONE PIECE OF ADVICE, WHAT WOULD IT BE?

Save every single action figure, every single comic book you get, because as an adult you will spend massive amounts of time and money reacquiring them. Seriously though, I would tell him no matter how dark it gets, no matter how much you may feel alone, it all gets better. Keep drawing, keep dreaming, and, above all, believe in yourself. Don't worry that you are not really good at any sports. Everything that you may get teased for or made fun of for will not only be accepted, it will help you achieve more than you ever could imagine.

First Nation Flavor
Chef Bear Robe's recipe for success

Chef: Aaron Joseph Bear Robe.

Age: 30.

Tribe: Blackfoot.

Signature: Traditional Aboriginal foods with a contemporary twist.

Philosophy: "You can't place something inside of a time capsule and be relevant," says Robe. "It becomes a novelty. You need to push food forward."

Résumé: Robe has graced the kitchens of a number of foodie-favorite restaurants, including Toronto's Splendido, Calgary's River Café, and his own Native-centric Keriwa Café.

Story: Robe was exposed to traditional Aboriginal food from an early age. He grew up on the Siksika Nation reserve in Alberta and eventually moved to Calgary in his teenage years, where he began working his way up in the kitchen. Ready to take the reins on his own projects, Robe eventually made the move to Toronto, where he's been ever since.

Cultural Influence: "People got together for traditional ceremonies. There would be a lot of stews in the stove: really simple, hearty austere food like potatoes, fry bread, bannock, bologna sandwiches on white bread," says Robe. "I was just trying to recapture those flavors—those flavors you can taste and you can smell."

■ Braised Bison Tongue Pemmican

Drawing on two traditional Native dishes—bison and pemmican—Robe fuses the two in a modern presentation, adding a sweeter braise and berry sauce. Bison or beef tongue, certainly, represents a more contemporary, daring palate as well.

HOOP BREAKING

Hip hop/cultural dancer **James Jones** (Cree from Tall Cree First Nation) shares stories of his success.

James mixes break dancing with traditional hoop dancing to create his own unique style of dance. He was the first Aboriginal street dancer to make it to the finals of *So You Think You Can Dance Canada*. Now he tours the world performing with stars like Maestro Fresh Wes, Snoop Dogg, and A Tribe Called Red. Crazy.

Starting Out

I started dancing when I was six years old. I was obsessed with the old rap videos of MC Hammer and Michael Jackson and used to perform their party dances. I used to enter these little weekly competitions in the little town by my reserve. I moved to Edmonton when I was nine, and I met a bunch of Aboriginal break-dancers who'd already been in the dance scene for quite a few years.

When I was about thirteen, I started getting into powwow dancing. I had a few friends who were break-dancers but also powwow dancers. One of them took me under his wing. He was organizing a tour of Europe for a powwow group. And one of the dancers dropped out, so he took me. That's where I actually learned about First Nations powwow dancing on the road, on tour in Europe.

Making History on *So You Think You Can Dance Canada*

I don't watch TV. I didn't even know what *So You Think You Can Dance Canada* was. I had a few dancer friends who kidnapped me and forced me to go to the audition in Calgary. I did the audition for fun. And I ended up going to the finals in Toronto. It was such a crazy experience and really opened my eyes to the dance world.

Grad
JUST THE BEGINNING

Sure, we can scoff at it, say it isn't that big of a deal, but it is. It's about an accomplishment that many struggle to see. It's about transition. It's about shedding the years of high school and turning into the adult you are meant to be. It's about wearing a hot-pink dress…

Sweetmoon Photography
a.k.a. **Tenille Campbell**
(Déné, English River First Nation, Métis)

Zach (Déné, English River First Nation)
What's Next: University of Regina, Nursing

Janine (Métis) | **What's Next:** Bachelor of Education and hoping to become a marine biologist in the future

Follow the desires of your heart, do not be afraid to be the real you because you hold the key to your happiness.

Lucas (Déné, English River First Nation)
What's Next: Carpentry apprenticeship

Shaniya (Déné, English River First Nation)

*No one can take learning away from me and
the world around me is my teacher . . . I won't
look back . . . I'll keep on going forward . . .
Life is a journey by taking one step at a time.*

Jaydon (Déné, English River First Nation, Métis) | **Fave Memory:** Playing hockey

Brianna (Déné, English River First Nation) | **What's Next:** College for hairstyling

Painting by Kit Thomas (Iroquois St. Regis Mohawk)

Weaving Dreams

Patricia Stein
(Lakota)

"Broken hoop."
Oh, but I see it whole.

Every bend breaks a barrier that's held us below.

Ends bound with love,
The kind without checks.

Fractions forced upon us,
Time to take a step.

A step for our future,
Those seven generations . . .
My grandchildren will not know of these situations.

Every knot a prayer,
A silent healing in the air.

Reworking our web to bring us there,
There in a place where our ancestors dance.

Every circle woven brings us closer yet . . .
Tie the last knot,
No longer distraught.

Our dreams will come through,
Dropping the bad with the morning dew.

About the Contributors

CHRISTIAN ALLAIRE (Ojibway from Nipissing First Nation and French-Italian) is a freelance writer and assistant stylist based in Toronto. He has been published in the *National Post*, *Interview*, *Flare*, *Maisonneuve* and the *Toronto Star*. He wears a lot of black and is deathly afraid of owls.

KRISTINA BAD HAND (Sicangu Lakota and Cherokee) is an illustrator with a love of all arts. Her love of superheroes led her to become a comic book artist dedicated to showing diversity in comics and bringing positive role models back to today's youth.

CHRISTI BELCOURT (Métis) is a visual artist whose work explores and celebrates the beauty of the natural world. Her work is found in the permanent collections of galleries and museums across Canada, including the Canadian Museum of History and the National Gallery of Canada.

JOSEPH BOYDEN (Anishinaabe) is an internationally acclaimed writer, who has received numerous awards for his novels including the McNally Robinson Aboriginal Book of the Year and the Scotiabank Giller Prize. He is currently a lecturer with the University of British Columbia Creative Writing Program. He divides his time between New Orleans and Ontario.

ASHLEY CALLINGBULL (Enoch Cree Nation) appears in the TV series *Blackstone* and is currently enrolled at the Northern Alberta Institute of Technology in the Television program. In 2010, Ashley placed second runner-up in the Miss Universe Canada Pageant and continues to speak around the globe. In 2011, Ashley received the Dreamcatcher Role Model Award.

NICOLA CAMPBELL (Nle7kepmx [Thompson], Nsilx [Okanagan], and Métis) is an award-winning author who writes adult and children's fiction, non-fiction, and poetry. She recently completed a MFA in Writing from the University of British Columbia, where she is also currently pursuing a MA in Indigenous Studies.

TENILLE CAMPBELL (English River First Nation (Déné) and Métis) is a writer and photographer. After completing an MFA at the University of British Columbia, she moved to Saskatoon, Saskatchewan, and started her business, Sweetmoon Photography. She is currently pursuing her PhD, specializing in Aboriginal Literature, from the University of Saskatchewan.

KELLI CLIFTON (Tsimshian) is a recent graduate of the Visual Arts program at the University of Victoria. She attends the Freda Diesing School of Northwest Coast Art in Terrace, British Columbia.

ANTHONY "THOSH" COLLINS (Pima from Salt River, Seneca-Cayuga) is a photographer based out of Arizona. He has studied at the San Francisco Art Institute. He is a huge advocate for healthy living and sits on the board for the Native Wellness Institute, a nonprofit that creates wellness programs for communities throughout Native country.

CONLIN DELBAERE-SAWCHUK (Métis) cultivated his passion for music from an early age. In 2010, he completed his Bachelor of Music in classical voice performance at the University of Ottawa. Along with his siblings in the Métis Fiddler Quartet, he enjoys performing and sharing the Métis music tradition with audiences across Canada and beyond.

KARINA RAIN DOMINGUEZ (Hopi, Navajo, and of Mayan descent from Guatemala) is a writer and activist based out of Los Angeles. She works with the organization Pathways, assisting young woman from disadvantaged backgrounds in getting an education and becoming independent.

KEESIC DOUGLAS (Ojibway from Mnjikaning First Nation) is a photographer, filmmaker, and artist based out of Toronto. He completed his BFA in Photography at OCAD University and his MFA in Photography at the University of British Columbia. He currently works as an Assistant Professor and Interim Chair of the Indigenous Visual Culture program at OCAD University.

BUNKY ECHO-HAWK (Pawnee and Yakama) is a graduate of the Institute of American Indian Arts. He is a graphic designer, photographer, writer, and fine artist whose work has been exhibited across the United States and internationally. In 2006, Bunky co-founded NVision, a nonprofit collective of Native American artists, musicians, community organizers, and nonprofit professionals who focus on Native American youth empowerment.

THE EDD GIRLS are artists and sisters from the Diné Nation. Ruthie (19), Sierra (17), Chamisa (13), and Santana (11) have been making, showing, and selling their art since they were young children.

JP GLADU (Ojibwa, Sand Point First Nation) is the President and CEO for the Canadian Council for Aboriginal Business, based out of Toronto, Ontario. He was born and raised in Thunder Bay, Ontario, completed a forestry technician diploma in 1993, and obtained an undergraduate degree from Northern Arizona University in 2000. He also holds an Executive MBA from Queen's University.

CLAUDINE GLADUE is a Plains Cree Computer Science student finishing her degree at MacEwan University in Edmonton, Alberta.

LOUIE GONG (Nooksack, Squamish, Chinese, French, Scottish) is the founder of Eighth Generation, through which he merges traditional Coast Salish art with icons from popular culture. He is also an internationally recognized leader in the discourse around racial and cultural identity who has provided commentary for *NBC Nightly News*, the *New York Times* and MSNBC.com. His unique merger of art and activism has been featured in two documentary films, *Unreserved: the work of Louie Gong* (2010) and *Schuhe Machen Leute* (2013).

THOMAS GREYEYES is an interdisciplinary artist from the Navajo Nation. He majored in Intermedia at Arizona State University and has taught media and studio art college classes and youth mural workshops. Tom also participated in the acclaimed Artist Residency programs at ASU and the School of Unity and Liberation in Oakland, California.

DAVID GROULX (Ojibwe) is an award-winning poet from Northern Ontario. His poetry has appeared in numerous magazines around the world. He currently lives in a log home near Ottawa, Ontario.

JESSICA ROSEMARY HARJO is an enrolled member of the Otoe-Missouria Tribe of Oklahoma. She is also Osage, Pawnee, and Sac & Fox. Originally from Fairfax, Oklahoma (part of the Osage Reservation), she is now a PhD student at the University of Minnesota Graduate School of Design.

LAURALEE HARRIS is an artist who hails from the Sioux, Cree, Chipewyan, Montagnais, Ojibwe, Assiniboine First Nations, mixed with French, Irish, and English. Her unique, award-winning work has been exhibited across North America. Her groundbreaking technique has been incorporated into high school and university curricula and has been featured in the documentary *From the Spirit* (2009).

LIA HART currently lives in Vancouver but her home is in Masset, Haida Gwaii. She is a student at the University of British Columbia, and a student of the world. She wants to study rural Aboriginal Medicine.

HENRY HEAVY SHIELD is a proud member of the Kainai (Blood) First Nation. Originally from southern Alberta, Henry is currently based in Vancouver where he is working on his MA in English Literature, with an emphasis on Native literatures, from the University of British Columbia.

DANA HILLESTAD (Lakota) is an enrolled member of Sisseton Wahpeton Oyate, Sisseton, South Dakota. She lives in Atlanta, Georgia, and Oregon. Along with writing and her children, she devotes her time to the preservation of the Lahkóta and Dakota and Powhatan languages.

HEATHER HILLS, a.k.a. SOKOLUM, (Déné) is a makeup artist, hair stylist, cosmetics collector, nail lacquer wearer, and hair enthusiast. She is a YouTuber based out of Montreal, Quebec.

WANEEK HORN-MILLER is an Aboriginal advocate and Olympic athlete from the Kahnawake Mohawk territory. She is currently working with the Assembly of First Nations as the IndigenACTION Ambassador, to develop a National Indigenous sport, fitness, and wellness strategy, and has teamed up with the Aboriginal Peoples' Television Network and health experts to launch a fitness and healthy-eating initiative called Working It Out Together.

JAMES JONES (Tall Cree First Nation) takes time out from hoop dancing and touring to inspire youth through Dreams in Motion, a program that was created to empower youth across the country through interactive workshops and high energy performances. He lives in Edmonton, Alberta.

DAVID KILABUK (Inuk) is a self-taught photographer born and raised in Pangnirtung, Nunavut. He spends his free time photographing the spectacular landscapes, great people, and amazing wildlife of his home.

ISABELLE KNOCKWOOD is a Mi'kmaw Elder living on the Indian Brook First Nation reserve. She is a survivor of the Indian Residential School at Shubenacadie, Nova Scotia. She returned to school to finish her education at the age of 59, receiving a BA and pursuing a Masters at St. Mary's University, Halifax, Nova Scotia. In 2013, she received an Honorary Doctorate in Civil Law from St. Mary's University.

NADYA KWANDIBENS is Ojibwe (Anishinaabe) and French from the Northwest Angle # 37 First Nation in Ontario, Canada. She is a self-taught photographer specializing in natural light portraiture, event, and concert photography.

CHARLOTTE "SKARUIANEWAH" LOGAN is from the Akwesasne Mohawk Territory that straddles the U.S./Canadian border. She has for the past 10 years worked in the competitive field of RNA Molecular Biology Research in New York and Boston, while at the same time receiving a Masters in Molecular Biology at Brandeis University. She now resides in Onondaga Nation Territory and works for the Two Row Wampum Renewal Campaign.

CHAYLA DELORME MARACLE (Cree from Cowessess First Nation Saskatchewan and Mohawk from Tyendinaga Mohawk Territory) is a talented Jingle Dress Dancer and a fourth-year student at the University of Alberta, where she is majoring in Psychology and minoring in Native Studies.

ALANA MCLEOD (Cree, Scottish) comes from a family of fur traders, wilderness tour guides, hunters, and quilt makers. Her textile art reflects her heritage as a person of the north of Aboriginal descent.

RYAN MCMAHON (Anishinaabe) is a graduate of the prestigious Second City Conservatory in Toronto. Ryan's comedy focuses on the good, the bad, and the ugly of the collision between Indian Country and the mainstream.

ZACH MEDICINE SHIELD (Blackfoot from Siksika Nation) is an artist based in Alberta, Canada. A known advocate for alternative art forms, his style and taste are shaped by the horror, thriller, noir, and science fiction genres. His first full-length novel, *A Dream*, is in the works for release in 2014.

DEREK MILLER (Mohawk Six Nations) is an award-winning guitarist, singer, and songwriter. He began in career touring with Buffy Sainte-Marie and has gone on to win three Juno awards and a Canadian Aboriginal Music Award for his solo work.

SHARIA MUSTATIA is a Métis/Cree/French/Romanian writer and artist living in Vancouver, Coast Salish Territory. You might catch Sharai out on the street taking pictures, with her little dog along for the ride in a doggy backpack, as she awaits the publication of her first book.

MACHESHUU NEEDGANAGWEDGIN is Cree and a member of the Constance Lake First Nations Treaty 9 in Ontario. He is in grade 3 and attends Prince Charles Elementary School in Edmonton, Alberta.

DEREK NEPINAK (Saulteaux) has had a varied and challenging career, excelling as an athlete, youth care worker, lawyer, and Chief of the Pine Creek First Nation. In 2011, he was elected the Grand Chief of The Assembly of Manitoba Chiefs.

DENISE PAYETTE is a member of the Missisauga First Nation and attends Laurentian University in Sudbury, Ontario.

KIM PETERSON (Kwakwa_ka_'wakw from 'Namgis First Nation) is an energy projects coordinator for the 'Namgis First Nation. He completed his Natural Resource Technologist diploma with Nicola Valley Institute of Technology (NVIT).

COURTNEY POWLESS (Mohawk) lives and writes in Ottawa. A communications professional by day and a poet by night, Courtney sees storytelling as a cultural responsibility. Through stories, she says, we remember who we are, and we seed down new roots/routes.

DUKE REDBIRD (Ojibwa, Saugeen First Nation) is a poet, scholar, storyteller, inspirational speaker, and television personality. He was the first Aboriginal advisor/mentor at OCAD University and is a Fellow of McLaughlin College at York University. Duke's poetry has been published in numerous collections and anthologies across Canada and the United States.

AARON JOSEPH BEAR ROBE (Blackfoot from Siksika) was the owner and chef of the acclaimed Keriwa Café, a Native Canadian restaurant in Toronto. He has recently launched a new venture in the city, the Wine Academy social club.

PRISCELLA ROSE lives in Attawapiskat. She is a hairstylist, and wants to become a paramedic. Her hobbies are photojournalism, designing tattoos, painting, DJing, and broomball. She teaches a basic photography course and manages the James Bay Photography Facebook page.

MARTIN SENSMEIER is a model, actor, spoken word artist, and youth advocate. He grew up in Yakutat, Alaska, and belongs to the Tlingit and Koyukon-Athabascan Tribes.

JULIA SHAW is a Cree (Peepeekisis Nation) student at the University of Calgary.

RAQUEL SIMARD is from Winnipeg, Manitoba. She is a descendant of the Manigotagan Métis and the Oji-Cree First Nations of Island Lake.

ALIDA KINNIE STARR (Mixed Blood Mohawk) is an MC, Juno Award-winning producer, poet, and visual artist. She was awarded "Pioneer in Hip Hop" at Toronto's Manifesto Hip Hop Summit in 2011.

ARIGON STARR (Kickapoo and Muscogee Creek-Cherokee-Seneca) is a musician, actor, singer, songwriter, artist, and playwright based in Los Angeles, California. She is a founding member of the Indigenous Narratives Collective, a group of Native American comic creators.

KRIS STATNYK is Ch'ichyàa (Wolf Clan) from the Vuntut Gwitchin First Nation in Old Crow, Yukon Territory. He is currently a guest in Coast Salish Territory where he practices oonjit (white man) law in Vancouver, British Columbia.

PATTY STEIN (Lakota, Mexica, and German descent from North Dakota) is a veterinary tech turned Jill of All Trades currently based out of Olympia, Washington. She is the founder and head instructor at Arming Sisters (armingsisters.org), an organization utilizing self defense as a tool to bring about empowerment, self love, and ownership of body to Indigenous women across the United States and Canada.

AJA SY (Ojibway, Anishinaabe) is 11 years old and in Grade 6 at Edmison Heights Public School in Peterborough, Ontario. She enjoys hanging out with her friends, surfing social media, swimming, and spending time in the sugar bush.

TANYA TAGAQ GILLIS (Inuk) is an internationally renowned singer. Fusing her love of contemporary music and the ancient art form of throat singing, she has created her own unique solo style.

ADRIANE TAILFEATHERS is a member of the Blackfeet tribe located in Montana. She is currently pursuing a degree in Secondary Education—History and Political Science, and hopes to make a difference on the reservation.

KIT THOMAS (Iroquois, St. Regis Mohawk) studied art at the Pratt Institute in Brooklyn, New York. Her art is a fusion of cartoon, surreal, symbolic, and abstract styles, and her Native roots.

MICHELLE THRUSH (Cree) is a Gemini Award-winning actress. She lives in Calgary, Alberta, with her daughters, and is kept busy with her roles in the TV shows *Blackstone* and *Arctic Air*, and her workshop and performance work with youth. Her movie with Benicio del Toro, *Jimmy P: Psychotherapy of a Plains Indian*, premiered at the Cannes Film Festival.

FAITH TURNER is a Moose Cree First Nation member born and raised in Edmonton, Alberta. Faith lives with her husband and three children on her home reserve on Moose Factory Island, located in James Bay, Ontario.

JEFFREY VEREGGE (Port Gamble S'Kallam Tribe and Suquamish/Duwamish) is an award-winning writer and artist whose work has been exhibited across the United States. He graduated from the Art Institute of Seattle and is the lead designer/studio manager for a media agency that specializes in nonprofits.

TONYA-LEAH WATTS is an Odawa youth from Wikwemikong Unceded Indian Reserve on Manitoulin Island. She works hard to get good marks in school so that she can fulfill her dreams of becoming a doctor and a published writer.

SHANNON WEBB-CAMPBELL is a member of the Qualipu Mik'Maq Federation of Newfoundland Indians. She is working on her MFA in Creative Writing via the University of British Columbia's Optional Residency program, and lives in Halifax.

ABIGAIL WHITEYE (Moravian Delaware First Nation) attends high school in Sarnia, Ontario, and is passionate about playing basketball.

JADE WILLOUGHBY (Ojibway, Jamaican) is a Whitesand First Nation member and was born and raised in Thunder Bay, Ontario. She is contracted to the prestigious Wilhelmina Models agency and now lives in New York.

DARRELL YAZZIE, JR. was born and raised in Arizona, on the Navajo Nation, in a little town called Klagetoh. His hobbies are photography and painting. He attends college, pursuing a career as a veterinarian.

About the Editors

LISA CHARLEYBOY is a storyteller living in Toronto, who has a background in fashion and a heart in all things Indigenous. She has written about everything from Native appropriations, to pop culture, to politics, and has been named one of Toronto's top bloggers and one of Canada's top ten fashion bloggers. Recently she's been touted by *The Huffington Post* as one of three Aboriginal millennials to watch, and has received a Toronto DiverseCity Fellowship for 2013–2014.

With over eight years as a published writer, she has written for publications such as *The Guardian*, CBC Arts, *This Magazine*, *Spirituality & Health*, *Job Postings*, and *Spirit Magazine*. Before finishing her Bachelor of Arts, with Honors, in Professional Writing at York University, she was fortunate enough to have already had her own fashion column at Williams Lake Tribune. She has worked as a fashion editor at *Excalibur*, a fashion intern at *Lush* magazine, a weekly contributor at MSN.ca on beauty, fashion, and lifestyle, and a fashion columnist for *Indian Country Today*.

Lisa loves storytelling and enjoys every platform where she's able to share stories from the heart. She has just launched *Urban Native Magazine*, which is a Native lifestyle magazine geared toward inspiring Indigenous youth with positive success stories.

MARY BETH LEATHERDALE has been lucky enough to make a career out of reading and learning, having written, edited, and consulted on hundreds of books, magazines, and digital resources for children and youth. She has edited over a dozen anthologies, including iLit Digital Collection, original works by contemporary Canadian writers for youth. Before becoming the editorial director for Owlkids' magazine and book divisions in 2006, she was the editor of award-winning magazines *Chirp* and *OWL*.

Mary Beth's interest in Native culture developed while attending Howard Harwich Moravian Public School (now the Naahi Ridge Public School) with students from the Delaware Nation. After completing her Honors BA in Visual Arts at The University of Western Ontario, she went on to pursue a Master of Education in the Sociology of Education from the Ontario Institute of Studies in Education (OISE), where her research focused on the delivery of anti-racist curricula.

Mary Beth lives in Toronto with her family.